EXCELSIOR/REGENTS COLLEGE EXAMINATIONS

C000088884

THIS IS YOUR **PASSBOOK**® FOR ...

HEALTH I: PERSONAL HEALTH, PHYSICAL ASPECTS

NATIONAL LEARNING CORPORATION®
passbooks.com

PASSBOOK® SERIES

THE *PASSBOOK® SERIES* has been created to prepare applicants and candidates for the ultimate academic battlefield – the examination room.

At some time in our lives, each and every one of us may be required to take an examination – for validation, matriculation, admission, qualification, registration, certification, or licensure.

Based on the assumption that every applicant or candidate has met the basic formal educational standards, has taken the required number of courses, and read the necessary texts, the *PASSBOOK® SERIES* furnishes the one special preparation which may assure passing with confidence, instead of failing with insecurity. Examination questions – together with answers – are furnished as the basic vehicle for study so that the mysteries of the examination and its compounding difficulties may be eliminated or diminished by a sure method.

This book is meant to help you pass your examination provided that you qualify and are serious in your objective.

The entire field is reviewed through the huge store of content information which is succinctly presented through a provocative and challenging approach – the question-and-answer method.

A climate of success is established by furnishing the correct answers at the end of each test.

You soon learn to recognize types of questions, forms of questions, and patterns of questioning. You may even begin to anticipate expected outcomes.

You perceive that many questions are repeated or adapted so that you can gain acute insights, which may enable you to score many sure points.

You learn how to confront new questions, or types of questions, and to attack them confidently and work out the correct answers.

You note objectives and emphases, and recognize pitfalls and dangers, so that you may make positive educational adjustments.

Moreover, you are kept fully informed in relation to new concepts, methods, practices, and directions in the field.

You discover that you arre actually taking the examination all the time: you are preparing for the examination by "taking" an examination, not by reading extraneous and/or supererogatory textbooks.

In short, this PASSBOOK®, used directedly, should be an important factor in helping you to pass your test.

NONTRADITIONAL EDUCATION

Students returning to school as adults bring more varied experience to their studies than do the teenagers who begin college shortly after graduating from high school. As a result, there are numerous programs for students with nontraditional learning curves. Hundreds of colleges and universities grant degrees to people who cannot attend classes at a regular campus or have already learned what the college is supposed to teach.

You can earn nontraditional education credits in many ways:
- Passing standardized exams
- Demonstrating knowledge gained through experience
- Completing campus-based coursework, and
- Taking courses off campus

Some methods of assessing learning for credit are objective, such as standardized tests. Others are more subjective, such as a review of life experiences.

With some help from four hypothetical characters – Alice, Vin, Lynette, and Jorge – this article describes nontraditional ways of earning educational credit. It begins by describing programs in which you can earn a high school diploma without spending 4 years in a classroom. The college picture is more complicated, so it is presented in two parts: one on gaining credit for what you know through course work or experience, and a second on college degree programs. The final section lists resources for locating more information.

Earning High School Credit

People who were prevented from finishing high school as teenagers have several options if they want to do so as adults. Some major cities have back-to-school programs that allow adults to attend high school classes with current students. But the more practical alternatives for most adults are to take the General Educational Development (GED) tests or to earn a high school diploma by demonstrating their skills or taking correspondence classes.

Of course, these options do not match the experience of staying in high school and graduating with one's friends. But they are viable alternatives for adult learners committed to meeting and, often, continuing their educational goals.

GED Program

Alice quit high school her sophomore year and took a job to help support herself, her younger brother, and their newly widowed mother. Now an adult, she wants to earn her high school diploma – and then go on to college. Because her job as head cook and her family responsibilities keep her busy during the day, she plans to get a high school equivalency diploma. She will study for, and take, the GED tests. Every year, about half a million adults earn their high school credentials this way. A GED diploma is accepted in lieu of a high school one by more than 90 percent of employers, colleges, and universities, so it is a good choice for someone like Alice.

The GED testing program is sponsored by the American Council on Education and State and local education departments. It consists of examinations in five subject areas: Writing, science, mathematics, social studies, and literature and the arts. The tests also measure skills such as analytical ability, problem solving, reading comprehension, and ability to understand and apply information. Most of the questions are multiple choice; the writing test includes an essay section on a topic of general interest.

Eligibility rules for taking the exams vary, but some states require that you must be at least 18. Tests are given in English, Spanish, and French. In addition to standard print, versions in large print, Braille, and audiocassette are also available. Total time allotted for the tests is 7 1/2 hours.

The GED tests are not easy. About one-fourth of those who complete the exams every year do not pass. Passing scores are established by administering the tests to a sample of graduating high school seniors. The minimum standard score is set so that about one-third of graduating seniors would not pass the tests if they took them.

Because of the difficulty of the tests, people need to prepare themselves to take them. Often, they start by taking the Official GED Practice Tests, usually available through a local adult education center. Centers are listed in your phone book's blue pages under "Adult Education," "Continuing Education," or "GED." Adult education centers also have information about GED preparation classes and self-study materials. Classes are generally arranged to accommodate adults' work schedules. National Learning Corporation publishes several study guides that aim to thoroughly prepare test-takers for the GED.

School districts, colleges, adult education centers, and community organizations have information about GED testing schedules and practice tests. For more information, contact them, your nearest GED testing center, or:

GED Testing Service
One Dupont Circle, NW, Suite 250
Washington, DC 20036-1163
1(800) 62-MY GED (626-9433)
(202) 939-9490

Skills Demonstration

Adults who have acquired high school level skills through experience might be eligible for the National External Diploma Program. This alternative to the GED does not involve any direct instruction. Instead, adults seeking a high school diploma must demonstrate mastery of 65 competencies in 8 general areas: Communication; computation; occupational preparedness; and self, social, consumer, scientific, and technological awareness.

Mastery is shown through the completion of the tasks. For example, a participant could prove competency in computation by measuring a room for carpeting, figuring out the amount of carpet needed, and computing the cost.

Before being accepted for the program, adults undergo an evaluation. Tests taken at one of the program's offices measure reading, writing, and mathematics abilities. A take-home segment includes a self-assessment of current skills, an individual skill evaluation, and an occupational interest and aptitude test.

Adults accepted for the program have weekly meetings with an assessor. At the meeting, the assessor reviews the participant's work from the previous week. If the task has not been completed properly, the assessor explains the mistake. Participants continue to correct their errors until they master each competency. A high school diploma is awarded upon proven mastery of all 65 competencies.

Fourteen States and the District of Columbia now offer the External Diploma Program. For more information, contact:

External Diploma Program
One Dupont Circle, NW, Suite 250
Washington, DC 20036-1193
(202) 939-9475

Correspondence and Distance Study

Vin dropped out of high school during his junior year because his family's frequent moves made it difficult for him to continue his studies. He promised himself at the time he dropped out that he would someday finish the courses needed for his diploma. For people like Vin, who prefer to earn a traditional diploma in a nontraditional way, there are about a dozen accredited courses of study for earning a high school diploma by correspondence, or distance study. The programs are either privately run, affiliated with a university, or administered by a State education department.

Distance study diploma programs have no residency requirements, allowing students to continue their studies from almost any location. Depending on the course of study, students need not be enrolled full time and usually have more flexible schedules for finishing their work. Selection of courses ranges from vo-tech to college prep, and some programs place different emphasis on the types of diplomas offered. University affiliated schools, for example, allow qualified students to take college courses along with their high school ones. Students can then apply the college credits toward a degree at that university or transfer them to another institution.

Taking courses by distance study is often more challenging and time consuming than attending classes, especially for adults who have other obligations. Success depends on each student's motivation. Students usually do reading assignments on their own. Written exercises, which they complete and send to an instructor for grading, supplement their reading material.

A list of some accredited high schools that offer diplomas by distance study is available free from the Distance Education and Training Council, formerly known as the National Home Study Council. Request the "DETC Directory of Accredited Institutions" from:

The Distance Education and Training Council
1601 18th Street, NW.
Washington, DC 20009-2529
(202) 234-5100

Some publications profiling nontraditional college programs include addresses and descriptions of several high school correspondence ones. See the Resources section at the end of this article for more information.

Getting College Credit For What You Know

Adults can receive college credit for prior coursework, by passing examinations, and documenting experiential learning. With help from a college advisor, nontraditional students should assess their skills, establish their educational goals, and determine the number of college credits they might be eligible for.

Even before you meet with a college advisor, you should collect all your school and training records. Then, make a list of all knowledge and abilities acquired through experience, no matter how irrelevant they seem to your chosen field. Next, determine your educational goals: What specific field do you wish to study? What kind of a degree do you want? Finally, determine how your past work fits into the field of study. Later on, you will evaluate educational programs to find one that's right for you.

People who have complex educational or experiential learning histories might want to have their learning evaluated by the Regents Credit Bank. The Credit Bank, operated by Regents College of the University of the State of New York, allows people to consolidate credits earned through college, experience, or other methods. Special assessments are available for Regents College enrollees whose knowledge in a specific field cannot be adequately evaluated by standardized exams. For more information, contact the Regents Credit Bank at:

Regents College
7 Columbia Circle
Albany, NY 12203-5159
(518) 464-8500

Credit For Prior College Coursework

When Lynette was in college during the 1970s, she attended several different schools and took a variety of courses. She did well in some classes and poorly in others. Now that she is a successful business owner and has more focus, Lynette thinks she should forget about her previous coursework and start from scratch. Instead, she should start from where she is.

Lynette should have all her transcripts sent to the colleges or universities of her choice and let an admissions officer determine which classes are applicable toward a degree. A few credits here and there may not seem like much, but they add up. Even if the subjects do not seem relevant to any major, they might be counted as elective credits toward a degree. And comparing the cost of transcripts with the cost of college courses, it makes sense to spend a few dollars per transcript for a chance to save hundreds, and perhaps thousands, of dollars in books and tuition.

Rules for transferring credits apply to all prior coursework at accredited colleges and universities, whether done on campus or off. Courses completed off campus, often called extended learning, include those available to students through independent study and correspondence. Many schools have extended learning programs; Brigham Young University, for example, offers more than 300 courses through its Department of Independent Study. One type of extended learning is distance learning, a form of correspondence study by technological means such as television, video and audio, CD-ROM, electronic mail, and computer tutorials. See the Resources section at the end of this article for more information about publications available from the National University Continuing Education Association.

Any previously earned college credits should be considered for transfer, no matter what the subject or the grade received. Many schools do not accept the transfer of courses graded below a C or ones taken more than a designated number of years ago. Some colleges and universities also have limits on the number of credits that can be transferred and applied toward a degree. But not all do. For example, Thomas Edison State College, New Jersey's State college for adults, accepts the transfer of all 120 hours of credit required for a baccalaureate degree – provided all the credits are transferred from regionally accredited schools, no more than 80 are at the junior college level, and the student's grades overall and in the field of study average out to C.

To assign credit for prior coursework, most schools require original transcripts. This means you must complete a form or send a written, signed request to have your transcripts released directly to a college or university. Once you have chosen the schools you want to apply to, contact the schools you attended before. Find out how much each transcript costs, and ask them to send your transcripts to the ones you are applying to. Write a letter that includes your name (and names used during attendance, if different) and dates of attendance, along with the names and addresses of the schools to which your transcripts should be sent. Include payment and mail to the registrar at the schools you have attended. The registrar's office will process your request and send an official transcript of your coursework to the colleges or universities you have designated.

Credit For Noncollege Courses

Colleges and universities are not the only ones that offer classes. Volunteer organizations and employers often provide formal training worth college credit. The American Council on Education has two programs that assess thousands of specific courses and make recommendations on the amount of college credit they are worth. Colleges and universities accept the recommendations or use them as guidelines.

One program evaluates educational courses sponsored by government agencies, business and industry, labor unions, and professional and voluntary organizations. It is the Program on Noncollegiate Sponsored Instruction (PONSI). Some of the training seminars Alice has participated in covered topics such as food preparation, kitchen safety, and nutrition. Although she has not yet earned her GED, Alice can earn college credit because of her completion of these formal job-training seminars. The number of credits each seminar is worth does not hinge on Alice's current eligibility for college enrollment.

The other program evaluates courses offered by the Army, Navy, Air Force, Marines, Coast Guard, and Department of Defense. It is the Military Evaluations Program. Jorge has never attended college, but the engineering technology classes he completed as part of his military training are worth college credit. And as an Army veteran, Jorge is eligible for a service that takes the evaluations one step further. The Army/American Council on Education Registry Transcript System (AARTS) will provide Jorge with an individualized transcript of American Council on Education credit recommendations for all courses he completed, the military occupational specialties (MOS's) he held, and examinations he passed while in the Army. All Army and National Guard enlisted personnel and veterans who enlisted after October 1981 are eligible for the transcript. Similar services are being considered by the Navy and Marine Corps.

To obtain a free transcript, see your Army Education Center for a 5454R transcript request form. Include your name, Social Security number, basic active service date, and complete address where you want the transcript sent. Mail your request to:
AARTS Operations Center
415 McPherson Ave.
Fort Leavenworth, KS 66027-1373

Recommendations for PONSI are published in *The National Guide to Educational Credit for Training Programs;* military program recommendations are in *The Guide to the Evaluation of Educational Experiences in the Armed Forces.* See the Resources section at the end of this article for more information about these publications.

Former military personnel who took a foreign language course through the Defense Language Institute may request course transcripts by sending their name, Social Security number, course title, duration of the course, and graduation date to:

Commandant, Defense Language Institute
Attn: ATFL-DAA-AR
Transcripts
Presidio of Monterey
Monterey, CA 93944-5006

Not all of Jorge's and Alice's courses have been assessed by the American Council on Education. Training courses that have no Council credit recommendation should still be assessed by an advisor at the schools they want to attend. Course descriptions, class notes, test scores, and other documentation may be helpful for comparing training courses to their college equivalents. An oral examination or other demonstration of competency might also be required.

There is no guarantee you will receive all the credits you are seeking – but you certainly won't if you make no attempt.

Credit By Examination

Standardized tests are the best-known method of receiving college credit without taking courses. These exams are often taken by high school students seeking advanced placement for college, but they are also available to adult learners. Testing programs and colleges and universities offer exams in a number of subjects. Two U.S. Government institutes have foreign language exams for employees that also may be worth college credit.

It is important to understand that receiving a passing score on these exams does not mean you get college credit automatically. Each school determines which test results it will accept, minimum scores required, how scores are converted for credit, and the amount of credit, if any, to be assigned. Most colleges and universities accept the American Council on Education credit recommendations, published every other year in the 250-page *Guide to Educational Credit by Examination*. For more information, contact:

The American Council on Education
Credit by Examination Program
One Dupont Circle, Suite 250
Washington, DC 20036-1193
(202) 939-9434

Testing programs:

You might know some of the five national testing programs by their acronyms or initials: CLEP, ACT PEP: RCE, DANTES, AP, and NOCTI. (The meanings of these initialisms are explained below.) There is some overlap among programs; for example, four of them have introductory accounting exams. Since you will not be awarded credit more than once for a specific subject, you should carefully evaluate each program for the subject exams you wish to take. And before taking an exam, make sure you will be awarded credit by the college or university you plan to attend.

CLEP (College-Level Examination Program), administered by the College Board, is the most widely accepted of the national testing programs; more than 2,800 accredited schools award credit for passing exam scores. Each test covers material taught in basic undergraduate courses. There are five general exams – English composition, humanities, college mathematics, natural sciences, and social sciences and history – and many subject exams. Most exams are entirely multiple-choice, but English composition exams may include an essay section. For more information, contact:

CLEP
P.O. Box 6600
Princeton, NJ 08541-6600
(609) 771-7865

ACT PEP: RCE (American College Testing Proficiency Exam Program: Regents College Examinations) tests are given in 38 subjects within arts and sciences, business, education, and nursing. Each exam is recommended for either lower- or upper-level credit. Exams contain either objective or extended response questions, and are graded according to a standard score, letter grade, or pass/fail. Fees vary, depending on the subject and type of exam. For more information or to request free study guides, contact:

ACT PEP: Regents College Examinations
P.O. Box 4014
Iowa City, IA 52243
(319) 337-1387
(New York State residents must contact Regents College directly.)

DANTES (Defense Activity for Nontraditional Education Support) standardized tests are developed by the Educational Testing Service for the Department of Defense. Originally administered only to military personnel, the exams have been available to the public since 1983. About 50 subject tests cover business, mathematics, social science, physical science, humanities, foreign languages, and applied technology. Most of the tests consist entirely of multiple-choice questions. Schools determine their own administering fees and testing schedules. For more information or to request free study sheets, contact:

DANTES Program Office
Mail Stop 31-X
Educational Testing Service
Princeton, NJ 08541
1(800) 257-9484

The AP (Advanced Placement) Program is a cooperative effort between secondary schools and colleges and universities. AP exams are developed each year by committees of college and high school faculty appointed by the College Board and assisted by consultants from the Educational Testing Service. Subjects include arts and languages, natural sciences, computer science, social sciences, history, and mathematics. Most tests are 2 or 3 hours long and include both multiple-choice and essay questions. AP courses are available to help students prepare for exams, which are offered in the spring. For more information about the Advanced Placement Program, contact:

Advanced Placement Services
P.O. Box 6671
Princeton, NJ 08541-6671
(609) 771-7300

NOCTI (National Occupational Competency Testing Institute) assessments are designed for people like Alice, who have vocational-technical skills that cannot be evaluated by other tests. NOCTI assesses competency at two levels: Student/job ready and teacher/experienced worker. Standardized evaluations are available for occupations such as auto-body repair, electronics, mechanical drafting, quantity food preparation, and upholstering. The tests consist of multiple-choice questions and a performance component. Other services include workshops, customized assessments, and pre-testing. For more information, contact:

NOCTI
500 N. Bronson Ave.
Ferris State University
Big Rapids, MI 49307
(616) 796-4699

Colleges and universities:

Many colleges and universities have credit-by-exam programs, through which students earn credit by passing a comprehensive exam for a course offered by the institution. Among the most widely recognized are the programs at Ohio University, the University of North Carolina, Thomas Edison State College, and New York University.

Ohio University offers about 150 examinations for credit. In addition, you may sometimes arrange to take special examinations in non-laboratory courses offered at Ohio University. To take a test for credit, you must enroll in the course. If you plan to transfer the credit earned, you also need written permission from an official at your school. Books and study materials are available, for a cost, through the university. Exams must be taken within 6 months of the enrollment date; most last 3 hours. You may arrange to take the exam off campus if you do not live near the university.

Ohio University is on the quarter-hour system; most courses are worth 4 quarter hours, the equivalent of 3 semester hours. For more information, contact:

Independent Study
Tupper Hall 302
Ohio University
Athens, OH 45701-2979
1(800) 444-2910
(614) 593-2910

The University of North Carolina offers a credit-by-examination option for 140 independent study (correspondence) courses in foreign languages, humanities, social sciences, mathematics, business administration, education, electrical and computer engineering, health administration, and natural sciences. To take an exam, you must request and receive approval from both the course instructor and the independent studies department. Exams must be taken within six months of enrollment, and you may register for no more than two at a time. If you are not near the University's Chapel Hill campus, you may take your exam under supervision at an accredited college, university, community college, or technical institute. For more information, contact:

Independent Studies
CB #1020, The Friday Center
UNC-Chapel Hill
Chapel Hill, NC 27599-1020
1(800) 862-5669 / (919) 962-1134

The Thomas Edison College Examination Program offers more than 50 exams in liberal arts, business, and professional areas. Thomas Edison State College administers tests twice a month in Trenton, New Jersey; however, students may arrange to take their tests with a proctor at any accredited American college or university or U.S. military base. Most of the tests are multiple choice; some also include short answer or essay questions. Time limits range from 90 minutes to 4 hours, depending on the exam. For more information, contact:

Thomas Edison State College
TECEP, Office of Testing and Assessment
101 W. State Street
Trenton, NJ 08608-1176
(609) 633-2844

New York University's Foreign Language Program offers proficiency exams in more than 40 languages, from Albanian to Yiddish. Two exams are available in each language: The 12-point test is equivalent to 4 undergraduate semesters, and the 16-point exam may lead to upper level credit. The tests are given at the university's Foreign Language Department throughout the year.

Proof of foreign language proficiency does not guarantee college credit. Some colleges and universities accept transcripts only for languages commonly taught, such as French and Spanish. Nontraditional programs are more likely than traditional ones to grant credit for proficiency in other languages.

For an informational brochure and registration form for NYU's foreign language proficiency exams, contact:

New York University
Foreign Language Department
48 Cooper Square, Room 107
New York, NY 10003
(212) 998-7030

Government institutes:

The Defense Language Institute and Foreign Service Institute administer foreign language proficiency exams for personnel stationed abroad. Usually, the tests are given at the end of intensive language courses or upon completion of service overseas. But some people – like Jorge, who knows Spanish – speak another language fluently and may be allowed to take a proficiency exam in that language before completing their tour of duty. Contact one of the offices listed below to obtain transcripts of those scores. Proof of proficiency does not guarantee college credit, however, as discussed above.

To request score reports from the Defense Language Institute for Defense Language Proficiency Tests, send your name, Social Security number, language for which you were tested, and, most importantly, when and where you took the exam to:

Commandant, Defense Language Institute
Attn: ATFL-ES-T
DLPT Score Report Request
Presidio of Monterey
Monterey, CA 93944-5006

To request transcripts of scores for Foreign Service Institute exams, send your name, Social Security number, language for which you were tested, and dates or year of exams to:

Foreign Service Institute
Arlington Hall
4020 Arlington Boulevard
Rosslyn, VA 22204-1500
Attn: Testing Office (Send your request to the attention of the testing office of the foreign language in which you were tested)

Credit For Experience

Experiential learning credit may be given for knowledge gained through job responsibilities, personal hobbies, volunteer opportunities, homemaking, and other experiences. Colleges and universities base credit awards on the knowledge you have attained, not for the experience alone. In addition, the knowledge must be college level; not just any learning will do. Throwing horseshoes as a hobby is not likely to be worth college credit. But if you've done research on how and where the sport originated, visited blacksmiths, organized tournaments, and written a column for a trade journal – well, that's a horseshoe of a different color.

Adults attempting to get credit for their experience should be forewarned: Having your experience evaluated for college credit is time-consuming, tedious work – not an easy shortcut for people who want quick-fix college credits. And not all experience, no matter how valuable, is the equivalent of college courses.

Requesting college credit for your experiential learning can be tricky. You should get assistance from a credit evaluations officer at the school you plan to attend, but you should also have a general idea of what your knowledge is worth. A common method for converting knowledge into credit is to use a college catalog. Find course titles and descriptions that match what you have learned through experience, and request the number of credits offered for those courses.

Once you know what credit to ask for, you must usually present your case in writing to officials at the college you plan to attend. The most common form of presenting experiential learning for credit is the portfolio. A portfolio is a written record of your knowledge along with a request for equivalent college credit. It includes an identification and description of the knowledge for which you are requesting credit, an explanatory essay of how the knowledge was gained and how it fits into your educational plans, documentation that you have acquired such knowledge, and a request for college credit. Required elements of a portfolio vary by schools but generally follow those guidelines.

In identifying knowledge you have gained, be specific about exactly what you have learned. For example, it is not enough for Lynette to say she runs a business. She must identify the knowledge she has gained from running it, such as personnel management, tax law, marketing strategy, and inventory review. She must also include brief descriptions about her knowledge of each to support her claims of having those skills.

The essay gives you a chance to relay something about who you are. It should address your educational goals, include relevant autobiographical details, and be well organized, neat, and convey confidence. In his essay, Jorge might first state his goal of becoming an engineer. Then he would explain why he joined the Army, where he got hands-on training and experience in developing and servicing electronic equipment.

This, he would say, led to his hobby of creating remote-controlled model cars, of which he has built 20. His conclusion would highlight his accomplishments and tie them to his desire to become an electronic engineer.

Documentation is evidence that you've learned what you claim to have learned. You can show proof of knowledge in a variety of ways, including audio or video recordings, letters from current or former employers describing your specific duties and job performance, blueprints, photographs or artwork, and transcripts of certifying exams for professional licenses and certification – such as Alice's certification from the American Culinary Federation. Although documentation can take many forms, written proof alone is not always enough. If it is impossible to document your knowledge in writing, find out if your experiential learning can be assessed through supplemental oral exams by a faculty expert.

Earning a College Degree

Nontraditional students often have work, family, and financial obligations that prevent them from quitting their jobs to attend school full time. Can they still meet their educational goals? Yes.

More than 150 accredited colleges and universities have nontraditional bachelor's degree programs that require students to spend little or no time on campus; over 300 others have nontraditional campus-based degree programs. Some of those schools, as well as most junior and community colleges, offer associate's degrees nontraditionally. Each school with a nontraditional course of study determines its own rules for awarding credit for prior coursework, exams, or experience, as discussed previously. Most have charges on top of tuition for providing these special services.

Several publications profile nontraditional degree programs; see the Resources section at the end of this article for more information. To determine which school best fits your academic profile and educational goals, first list your criteria. Then, evaluate nontraditional programs based on their accreditation, features, residency requirements, and expenses. Once you have chosen several schools to explore further, write to them for more information. Detailed explanations of school policies should help you decide which ones you want to apply to.

Get beyond the printed word – especially the glowing words each school writes about itself. Check out the schools you are considering with higher education authorities, alumni, employers, family members, and friends. If possible, visit the campus to talk to students and instructors and sit in on a few classes, even if you will be completing most or all of your work off campus. Ask school officials questions about such things as enrollment numbers, graduation rate, faculty qualifications, and confusing details about the application process or academic policies. After you have thoroughly investigated each prospective college or university, you can make an informed decision about which is right for you.

Accreditation

Accreditation is a process colleges and universities submit to voluntarily for getting their credentials. An accredited school has been investigated and visited by teams of observers and has periodic inspections by a private accrediting agency. The initial review can take two years or more.

Regional agencies accredit entire schools, and professional agencies accredit either specialized schools or departments within schools. Although there are no national accrediting standards, not just any accreditation will do. Countless "accreditation associations" have been invented by schools, many of which have no academic programs and sell phony degrees, to accredit themselves. But 6 regional and about 80 professional accrediting associations in the United States are recognized by the U.S. Department of Education or the Commission on Recognition of Postsecondary Accreditation. When checking accreditation, these are the names to look for. For more information about accreditation and accrediting agencies, contact:

Institutional Participation Oversight Service Accreditation and State Liaison Division
U.S. Department of Education
ROB 3, Room 3915
600 Independence Ave., SW
Washington, DC 20202-5244
(202) 708-7417

Because accreditation is not mandatory, lack of accreditation does not necessarily mean a school or program is bad. Some schools choose not to apply for accreditation, are in the process of applying, or have educational methods too unconventional for an accrediting association's standards. For the nontraditional student, however, earning a degree from a college or university with recognized accreditation is an especially important consideration. Although nontraditional education is becoming more widely accepted, it is not yet mainstream. Employers skeptical of a degree earned in a nontraditional manner are likely to be even less accepting of one from an unaccredited school.

Program Features

Because nontraditional students have diverse educational objectives, nontraditional schools are diverse in what they offer. Some programs are geared toward helping students organize their scattered educational credits to get a degree as quickly as possible. Others cater to those who may have specific credits or experience but need assistance in completing requirements. Whatever your educational profile, you should look for a program that works with you in obtaining your educational goals.

A few nontraditional programs have special admissions policies for adult learners like Alice, who plan to earn their GEDs but want to enroll in college in the meantime. Other features of nontraditional programs include individualized learning agreements, intensive academic counseling, cooperative learning and internship placement, and waiver of some prerequisites or other requirements – as well as college credit for prior coursework, examinations, and experiential learning, all discussed previously.

Lynette, whose primary goal is to finish her degree, wants to earn maximum credits for her business experience. She will look for programs that do not limit the number of credits awarded for equivalency exams and experiential learning. And since well-documented proof of knowledge is essential for earning experiential learning credits, Lynette should make sure the program she chooses provides assistance to students submitting a portfolio.

Jorge, on the other hand, has more credits than he needs in certain areas and is willing to forego some. To become an engineer, he must have a bachelor's degree; but because he is accustomed to hands-on learning, Jorge is interested in getting experience as he gains more technical skills. He will concentrate on finding schools with strong cooperative education, supervised fieldwork, or internship programs.

Residency Requirements

Programs are sometimes deemed nontraditional because of their residency requirements. Many people think of residency for colleges and universities in terms of tuition, with in-state students paying less than out-of-state ones. Residency also may refer to where a student lives, either on or off campus, while attending school.

But in nontraditional education, residency usually refers to how much time students must spend on campus, regardless of whether they attend classes there. In some nontraditional programs, students need not ever step foot on campus. Others require only a very short residency, such as one day or a few weeks. Many schools have standard residency requirements of several semesters but schedule classes for evenings or weekends to accommodate working adults.

Lynette, who previously took courses by independent study, prefers to earn credits by distance study. She will focus on schools that have no residency requirement. Several colleges and universities have nonresident degree completion programs for adults with some college credit. Under the direction of a faculty advisor, students devise a plan for earning their remaining credits. Methods for earning credits include independent study, distance learning, seminars, supervised fieldwork, and group study at arranged sites. Students may have to earn a certain number of credits through the degree-granting institution. But many programs allow students to take courses at accredited schools of their choice for transfer toward their degree.

Alice wants to attend lectures but has an unpredictable schedule. Her best course of action will be to seek out short residency programs that require students to attend seminars once or twice a semester. She can take courses that are televised and videotape them to watch when her schedule permits, with the seminars helping to ensure that she properly completes her coursework. Many colleges and universities with short residency requirements also permit students to earn some credits elsewhere, by whatever means the student chooses.

Some fields of study require classroom instruction. As Jorge will discover, few colleges and universities allow students to earn a bachelor's degree in engineering entirely through independent study. Nontraditional residency programs are designed to accommodate adults' daytime work schedules. Jorge should look for programs offering evening, weekend, summer, and accelerated courses.

Tuition and Other Expenses

The final decisions about which schools Alice, Jorge, and Lynette attend may hinge in large part on a single issue: Cost. And rising tuition is only part of the equation. Beginning with application fees and continuing through graduation fees, college expenses add up.

Traditional and nontraditional students have some expenses in common, such as the cost of books and other materials. Tuition might even be the same for some courses, especially for colleges and universities offering standard ones at unusual times. But for nontraditional programs, students may also pay fees for services such as credit or transcript review, evaluation, advisement, and portfolio assessment.

Students are also responsible for postage and handling or setup expenses for independent study courses, as well as for all examination and transcript fees for transferring credits. Usually, the more nontraditional the program, the more detailed the fees. Some schools charge a yearly enrollment fee rather than tuition for degree completion candidates who want their files to remain active.

Although tuition and fees might seem expensive, most educators tell you not to let money come between you and your educational goals. Talk to someone in the financial aid department of the school you plan to attend or check your library for publications about financial aid sources. The U.S. Department of Education publishes a guide to Federal aid programs such as Pell Grants, student loans, and work-study. To order the free 74-page booklet, *The Student Guide: Financial Aid from the U.S. Department of Education,* contact:

Federal Student Aid Information Center
P.O. Box 84
Washington, DC 20044
1 (800) 4FED-AID (433-3243)

Resources

Information on how to earn a high school diploma or college degree without following the usual routes is available from several organizations and in numerous publications. Information on nontraditional graduate degree programs, available for master's through doctoral level, though not discussed in this article, can usually be obtained from the same resources that detail bachelor's degree programs.

National Learning Corporation publishes study guides for all of these exams, for both general examinations and tests in specific subject areas. To order study guides, or to browse their catalog featuring more than 5,000 titles, visit NLC online at www.passbooks.com, or contact them by phone at (800) 632-8888.

Organizations

Adult learners should always contact their local school system, community college, or university to learn about programs that are readily available. The following national organizations can also supply information:

American Council on Education
One Dupont Circle
Washington, DC 20036-1193
(202) 939-9300

Within the American Council on Education, the Center for Adult Learning and Educational Credentials administers the National External Diploma Program, the GED Program, the Program on Noncollegiate Sponsored Instruction, the Credit by Examination Program, and the Military Evaluations Program.

EXCELSIOR/REGENTS COLLEGE EXAMINATIONS (E/RCE)

With Excelsior/Regents College Examinations, you can show what you know and earn the college-level credit you deserve. If you're like many adults today, you've worked hard to get where you are personally and professionally, and are working even harder to improve your situation. You're looking for a way to earn the college degree you've always wanted, and want your past training and experiences to apply toward that degree. Or perhaps you are interested in pursuing independent study in a subject for which Excelsior/Regents College Examinations offer credit. Either way, when you're ready, you can earn three or more credit hours with each Excelsior/Regents College Examination you take.

You don't have to be enrolled in Excelsior/Regents College to gain credit by examination. Credit earned by taking Excelsior/Regents College Examinations may be used at more than 900 other colleges and universities in the United States.

Excelsior/Regents College offers 32 highly respected degree programs for adult learners in Business, Liberal Arts, Nursing, and Technology. It's difficult for many adults to suspend life's everyday demands to go back to school. That's why the Excelsior/Regents College offers adult learners something unique—the opportunity to complete a degree without attending classes in a traditional college setting.

The Excelsior/Regents College degree programs combine independent study, classwork at colleges and universities throughout the world, coursework accomplished on the job, televised and Internet distance learning classes, and examinations for college credit like Excelsior/Regents College Examinations.

The Excelsior/Regents College specialize in providing adults a variety of ways to demonstrate the knowledge they've gained on the job or through past educational experiences and to earn college-level credit for it.

Excelsior/Regents College Examinations are college-level examinations that are used by more than 900 colleges and universities in the United States to award credit or advanced placement. Excelsior/Regents College Examinations provide flexible opportunities for adults to demonstrate their college-level knowledge in the arts and sciences, business, education, and nursing. They enable colleges to offer students options such as advanced placement and exemption from course requirements, and give employers a means to allow employees to earn credit toward job advancement or to pursue a college education without interrupting work schedules. Excelsior/Regents College Examinations credit has also been used toward teach certification or advancement and in fulfillment of civil service qualifications and continuing education requirements.

Registration

Registration materials for Excelsior/Regents College Examinations can be obtained by a variety of means. Detailed information about the administration of the exams, testing center locations, fees, provisions for international and reasonable accommodations testing, and complete instructions for registering are included in the free registration packet. Request the registration packet as follows:

Postal mail: The Administration
Regents College
7 Columbia Circle
Albany, New York 12203-5159

Telephone: 888-RCEXAMS

Fax: (518) 464-8777

E-mail: testadmin@regents.edu

TDD   (518) 464-8501

Web: www.regents.edu/804.htm

When you're ready to demonstrate what you've learned, you can complete the registration process by the traditional mail method or, for faster eligibility, register entirely by phone. Phone registration is very simple: Call 1-888-RCEXAMS, toll-free, to register using your credit card. Once your registration is complete, you will receive an Authorization to Test letter that will admit you to the Sylvan Technology Center you choose. You will have 90 days to schedule your exam by calling Sylvan directly, toll-free.

Test Development and Scoring

A committee of faculty determined the content to be tested on each Excelsior/Regents College examination. Committee members are teaching faculty and practicing professionals in the field covered by the exam. The Excelsior/Regents College Assessment Unit staff oversee the technical aspects of test construction in accordance with current professional standards.

Multiple-choice examinations may contain anywhere from 80 to 160 four-option multiple-choice questions, some of which are unscored, experimental questions. Extended response and mixed format examinations will have fewer questions that you must answer at some length. Since you will not be able to tell which questions are experimental, you should do your best on all of them. Scores are based on ability level as defined in the item response theory (IRT) method of examination development, rather than simply your total number of correct answers. Your score will be reported as a letter grade.

HEALTH I: PERSONAL HEALTH, PHYSICAL ASPECTS

Questions in the examination in Health I: Personal Health, Physical Aspects are based upon the areas of nutrition, first aid and safety, epidemiology, personal health, health observation, and health economics. The examination consists of objective questions and requires approximately 3 hours to complete.

OBJECTIVES

The candidate should be able to:

1. demonstrate knowledge of terminology, facts and trends in the physical aspects of personal health
2. demonstrate understanding of personal and physical health concepts, principles and procedures
3. assess individual health patterns
4. analyze, synthesize, and evaluate health knowledge, attitudes and behavior

CONTENT DESCRIPTION

Percentages shown in parentheses below indicate the amount of emphasis given to the topic in the examination.

I. Health Status (10%)
   A. The health examination
   B. Growth and development
      1. Stages
      2. Factors affecting
      3. Height-weight
      4. Body structure
   C. Physical fitness
      1. Relationship to total health
      2. Value of physical fitness
      3. Means of attaining physical fitness

II. Nutrition (20%)
   A. Basic four (content, quantity, quality)
   B. Food nutrients
      1. Energy producers
      2. Body regulators
   C. Fads and fallacies
      1. Diets
      2. Health food faddism
   D. Recommended dietary allowances
   E. Basal metabolism rates
      1. Definition
      2. Determination
      3. Influencing factors
      4. Total calorie usage
   F. Food processing and preparation
      1. Processing procedures
      2. Enrichment program
      3. Food additives
      4. Modification
      5. Food supplements
      6. Packaging and labeling
      7. Individual food preparation
   G. Dietary deficiency diseases
      1. Protein
      2. Vitamin
      3. Mineral
   H. Special nutritional needs
      1. Underweight—overweight—obesity
      2. Therapeutic diets

3. Age variation

III. Dental Health (7%)
   A. Functions of the teeth
   B. Care of the teeth
      1. Personal
      2. Professional
   C. Nutritional implication
   D. Dental programs
   E. Diseases of the teeth and supporting tissues
   F. Recent advances in dentistry

IV. Senses (8%)
   A. Vision
      1. Visual function and supporting structures
      2. Common vision tests
      3. Preventive eye care
      4. Eye disorders
      5. Corrective devices
      6. Education of the visually handicapped
   B. Hearing
      1. Function and supporting structures
      2. Common hearing tests
      3. Protection of the ear
      4. Prevention of hearing loss
      5. Hearing disorders
      6. Corrective devices
      7. Education of the handicapped
   C. Taste, smell, and touch
      1. Interrelationship with each other
      2. Their role in nutrition

V. The Individual's Role in Disease Protection and Prevention (20%)
   A. Communicable diseases
      1. Control of communicable diseases
         a. disease terminology
         b. causative agents
         c. disease transmission
         d. resistance
         e. immunity

2. Communicable disease problems
   a. respiratory diseases
   b. common communicable diseases
   c. venereal diseases
   d. other diseases

B. Chronic and degenerative diseases
  1. Contributory factors and causes
  2. Personal responsibility
  3. Classification

VI. Securing Health Services and Protection (15%)
  A. Evaluating health information
  B. Choosing health advisors
    1. Criteria for selection
    2. Sources of reliable information
    3. Medical and nonmedical specialists
  C. Medical economics and medical care programs
    1. Compulsory vs. voluntary programs
    2. Group medical practice
  D. Current problems in securing medical services
    1. Health manpower shortages and distribution
    2. Population distribution

VII. The Individual's Role in First Aid and Safety (20%)
  A. Foundations
    1. Values and purposes of first aid
    2. Legal implications
    3. Moral responsibility
    4. Incidence of accidents and injuries
    5. Principles of prevention
  B. Emergency priorities in first aid
    1. Serious bleeding
    2. Stoppage of breathing
    3. Traumatic shock
    4. Poisons
    5. Wounds and infections
    6. Sprains, strains, fractures, dislocations
  C. Safety
    1. Traffic and pedestrian
    2. Home and farm
    3. Fire
    4. School
    5. Recreational activities
    6. Disaster preparedness

HOW TO TAKE A TEST

You have studied long, hard and conscientiously.

With your official admission card in hand, and your heart pounding, you have been admitted to the examination room.

You note that there are several hundred other applicants in the examination room waiting to take the same test.

They all appear to be equally well prepared.

You know that nothing but your best effort will suffice. The "moment of truth" is at hand: you now have to demonstrate objectively, in writing, your knowledge of content and your understanding of subject matter.

You are fighting the most important battle of your life—to pass and/or score high on an examination which will determine your career and provide the economic basis for your livelihood.

What extra, special things should you know and should you do in taking the examination?

I. YOU MUST PASS AN EXAMINATION

A. WHAT EVERY CANDIDATE SHOULD KNOW
Examination applicants often ask us for help in preparing for the written test. What can I study in advance? What kinds of questions will be asked? How will the test be given? How will the papers be graded?

B. HOW ARE EXAMS DEVELOPED?
Examinations are carefully written by trained technicians who are specialists in the field known as "psychological measurement," in consultation with recognized authorities in the field of work that the test will cover. These experts recommend the subject matter areas or skills to be tested; only those knowledges or skills important to your success on the job are included. The most reliable books and source materials available are used as references. Together, the experts and technicians judge the difficulty level of the questions.

Test technicians know how to phrase questions so that the problem is clearly stated. Their ethics do not permit "trick" or "catch" questions. Questions may have been tried out on sample groups, or subjected to statistical analysis, to determine their usefulness.

Written tests are often used in combination with performance tests, ratings of training and experience, and oral interviews. All of these measures combine to form the best-known means of finding the right person for the right job.

II. HOW TO PASS THE WRITTEN TEST

A. BASIC STEPS

1) Study the announcement

How, then, can you know what subjects to study? Our best answer is: "Learn as much as possible about the class of positions for which you've applied." The exam will test the knowledge, skills and abilities needed to do the work.

Your most valuable source of information about the position you want is the official exam announcement. This announcement lists the training and experience qualifications. Check these standards and apply only if you come reasonably close to meeting them. Many jurisdictions preview the written test in the exam announcement by including a section called "Knowledge and Abilities Required," "Scope of the Examination," or some similar heading. Here you will find out specifically what fields will be tested.

2) Choose appropriate study materials

If the position for which you are applying is technical or advanced, you will read more advanced, specialized material. If you are already familiar with the basic principles of your field, elementary textbooks would waste your time. Concentrate on advanced textbooks and technical periodicals. Think through the concepts and review difficult problems in your field.

These are all general sources. You can get more ideas on your own initiative, following these leads. For example, training manuals and publications of the government agency which employs workers in your field can be useful, particularly for technical and professional positions. A letter or visit to the government department involved may result in more specific study suggestions, and certainly will provide you with a more definite idea of the exact nature of the position you are seeking.

3) Study this book!

III. KINDS OF TESTS

Tests are used for purposes other than measuring knowledge and ability to perform specified duties. For some positions, it is equally important to test ability to make adjustments to new situations or to profit from training. In others, basic mental abilities not dependent on information are essential. Questions which test these things may not appear as pertinent to the duties of the position as those which test for knowledge and information. Yet they are often highly important parts of a fair examination. For very general questions, it is almost impossible to help you direct your study efforts. What we can do is to point out some of the more common of these general abilities needed in public service positions and describe some typical questions.

1) General information

Broad, general information has been found useful for predicting job success in some kinds of work. This is tested in a variety of ways, from vocabulary lists to questions about current events. Basic background in some field of work, such as sociology or economics, may be sampled in a group of questions. Often these are principles which have become familiar to most persons through exposure rather than through formal training. It is difficult to advise you how to study for these questions; being alert to the world around you is our best suggestion.

2) Verbal ability

An example of an ability needed in many positions is verbal or language ability. Verbal ability is, in brief, the ability to use and understand words. Vocabulary and grammar tests are typical measures of this ability. Reading comprehension or paragraph interpretation questions are common in many kinds of civil service tests. You are given a paragraph of written material and asked to find its central meaning.

IV. KINDS OF QUESTIONS

1. Multiple-choice Questions

Most popular of the short-answer questions is the "multiple choice" or "best answer" question. It can be used, for example, to test for factual knowledge, ability to solve problems or judgment in meeting situations found at work.

A multiple-choice question is normally one of three types:
- It can begin with an incomplete statement followed by several possible endings. You are to find the one ending which *best* completes the statement, although some of the others may not be entirely wrong.
- It can also be a complete statement in the form of a question which is answered by choosing one of the statements listed.
- It can be in the form of a problem – again you select the best answer.

Here is an example of a multiple-choice question with a discussion which should give you some clues as to the method for choosing the right answer:

When an employee has a complaint about his assignment, the action which will *best* help him overcome his difficulty is to
A. discuss his difficulty with his coworkers
B. take the problem to the head of the organization
C. take the problem to the person who gave him the assignment
D. say nothing to anyone about his complaint

In answering this question, you should study each of the choices to find which is best. Consider choice "A" – Certainly an employee may discuss his complaint with fellow employees, but no change or improvement can result, and the complaint remains unresolved. Choice "B" is a poor choice since the head of the organization probably does not know what assignment you have been given, and taking your problem to him is known as "going over the head" of the supervisor. The supervisor, or person who made the assignment, is the person who can clarify it or correct any injustice. Choice "C" is, therefore, correct. To say nothing, as in choice "D," is unwise. Supervisors have and interest in knowing the problems employees are facing, and the employee is seeking a solution to his problem.

2. True/False

3. Matching Questions
Matching an answer from a column of choices within another column.

V. RECORDING YOUR ANSWERS

Computer terminals are used more and more today for many different kinds of exams.

For an examination with very few applicants, you may be told to record your answers in the test booklet itself. Separate answer sheets are much more common. If this separate answer sheet is to be scored by machine – and this is often the case – it is highly important that you mark your answers correctly in order to get credit.

VI. BEFORE THE TEST

YOUR PHYSICAL CONDITION IS IMPORTANT
If you are not well, you can't do your best work on tests. If you are half asleep, you can't do your best either. Here are some tips:

1) Get about the same amount of sleep you usually get. Don't stay up all night before the test, either partying or worrying—DON'T DO IT!
2) If you wear glasses, be sure to wear them when you go to take the test. This goes for hearing aids, too.
3) If you have any physical problems that may keep you from doing your best, be sure to tell the person giving the test. If you are sick or in poor health, you relay cannot do your best on any test. You can always come back and take the test some other time.

Common sense will help you find procedures to follow to get ready for an examination. Too many of us, however, overlook these sensible measures. Indeed, nervousness and fatigue have been found to be the most serious reasons why applicants fail to do their best on civil service tests. Here is a list of reminders:

- Begin your preparation early – Don't wait until the last minute to go scurrying around for books and materials or to find out what the position is all about.
- Prepare continuously – An hour a night for a week is better than an all-night cram session. This has been definitely established. What is more, a night a week for a month will return better dividends than crowding your study into a shorter period of time.
- Locate the place of the exam – You have been sent a notice telling you when and where to report for the examination. If the location is in a different town or otherwise unfamiliar to you, it would be well to inquire the best route and learn something about the building.
- Relax the night before the test – Allow your mind to rest. Do not study at all that night. Plan some mild recreation or diversion; then go to bed early and get a good night's sleep.
- Get up early enough to make a leisurely trip to the place for the test – This way unforeseen events, traffic snarls, unfamiliar buildings, etc. will not upset you.

- Dress comfortably – A written test is not a fashion show. You will be known by number and not by name, so wear something comfortable.
- Leave excess paraphernalia at home – Shopping bags and odd bundles will get in your way. You need bring only the items mentioned in the official notice you received; usually everything you need is provided. Do not bring reference books to the exam. They will only confuse those last minutes and be taken away from you when in the test room.
- Arrive somewhat ahead of time – If because of transportation schedules you must get there very early, bring a newspaper or magazine to take your mind off yourself while waiting.
- Locate the examination room – When you have found the proper room, you will be directed to the seat or part of the room where you will sit. Sometimes you are given a sheet of instructions to read while you are waiting. Do not fill out any forms until you are told to do so; just read them and be prepared.
- Relax and prepare to listen to the instructions
- If you have any physical problem that may keep you from doing your best, be sure to tell the test administrator. If you are sick or in poor health, you really cannot do your best on the exam. You can come back and take the test some other time.

VII. AT THE TEST

The day of the test is here and you have the test booklet in your hand. The temptation to get going is very strong. Caution! There is more to success than knowing the right answers. You must know how to identify your papers and understand variations in the type of short-answer question used in this particular examination. Follow these suggestions for maximum results from your efforts:

1) Cooperate with the monitor
The test administrator has a duty to create a situation in which you can be as much at ease as possible. He will give instructions, tell you when to begin, check to see that you are marking your answer sheet correctly, and so on. He is not there to guard you, although he will see that your competitors do not take unfair advantage. He wants to help you do your best.

2) Listen to all instructions
Don't jump the gun! Wait until you understand all directions. In most civil service tests you get more time than you need to answer the questions. So don't be in a hurry. Read each word of instructions until you clearly understand the meaning. Study the examples, listen to all announcements and follow directions. Ask questions if you do not understand what to do.

3) Identify your papers
Civil service exams are usually identified by number only. You will be assigned a number; you must not put your name on your test papers. Be sure to copy your number correctly. Since more than one exam may be given, copy your exact examination title.

4) Plan your time
Unless you are told that a test is a "speed" or "rate of work" test, speed itself is usually not important. Time enough to answer all the questions will be provided, but this

does not mean that you have all day. An overall time limit has been set. Divide the total time (in minutes) by the number of questions to determine the approximate time you have for each question.

5) Do not linger over difficult questions

If you come across a difficult question, mark it with a paper clip (useful to have along) and come back to it when you have been through the booklet. One caution if you do this – be sure to skip a number on your answer sheet as well. Check often to be sure that you have not lost your place and that you are marking in the row numbered the same as the question you are answering.

6) Read the questions

Be sure you know what the question asks! Many capable people are unsuccessful because they failed to *read* the questions correctly.

7) Answer all questions

Unless you have been instructed that a penalty will be deducted for incorrect answers, it is better to guess than to omit a question.

8) Speed tests

It is often better NOT to guess on speed tests. It has been found that on timed tests people are tempted to spend the last few seconds before time is called in marking answers at random – without even reading them – in the hope of picking up a few extra points. To discourage this practice, the instructions may warn you that your score will be "corrected" for guessing. That is, a penalty will be applied. The incorrect answers will be deducted from the correct ones, or some other penalty formula will be used.

9) Review your answers

If you finish before time is called, go back to the questions you guessed or omitted to give them further thought. Review other answers if you have time.

10) Return your test materials

If you are ready to leave before others have finished or time is called, take ALL your materials to the monitor and leave quietly. Never take any test material with you. The monitor can discover whose papers are not complete, and taking a test booklet may be grounds for disqualification.

VIII. EXAMINATION TECHNIQUES

1) Read the general instructions carefully. These are usually printed on the first page of the exam booklet. As a rule, these instructions refer to the timing of the examination; the fact that you should not start work until the signal and must stop work at a signal, etc. If there are any *special* instructions, such as a choice of questions to be answered, make sure that you note this instruction carefully.

2) When you are ready to start work on the examination, that is as soon as the signal has been given, read the instructions to each question booklet, underline any key words or phrases, such as *least, best, outline, describe*

and the like. In this way you will tend to answer as requested rather than discover on reviewing your paper that you *listed without describing*, that you selected the *worst* choice rather than the *best* choice, etc.

3) If the examination is of the objective or multiple-choice type – that is, each question will also give a series of possible answers: A, B, C or D, and you are called upon to select the best answer and write the letter next to that answer on your answer paper – it is advisable to start answering each question in turn. There may be anywhere from 50 to 100 such questions in the three or four hours allotted and you can see how much time would be taken if you read through all the questions before beginning to answer any. Furthermore, if you come across a question or group of questions which you know would be difficult to answer, it would undoubtedly affect your handling of all the other questions.

4) If the examination is of the essay type and contains but a few questions, it is a moot point as to whether you should read all the questions before starting to answer any one. Of course, if you are given a choice – say five out of seven and the like – then it is essential to read all the questions so you can eliminate the two that are most difficult. If, however, you are asked to answer all the questions, there may be danger in trying to answer the easiest one first because you may find that you will spend too much time on it. The best technique is to answer the first question, then proceed to the second, etc.

5) Time your answers. Before the exam begins, write down the time it started, then add the time allowed for the examination and write down the time it must be completed, then divide the time available somewhat as follows:
   • If 3-1/2 hours are allowed, that would be 210 minutes. If you have 80 objective-type questions, that would be an average of 2-1/2 minutes per question. Allow yourself no more than 2 minutes per question, or a total of 160 minutes, which will permit about 50 minutes to review.
   • If for the time allotment of 210 minutes there are 7 essay questions to answer, that would average about 30 minutes a question. Give yourself only 25 minutes per question so that you have about 35 minutes to review.

6) The most important instruction is to *read each question* and make sure you know what is wanted. The second most important instruction is to *time yourself properly* so that you answer every question. The third most important instruction is to *answer every question*. Guess if you have to but include something for each question. Remember that you will receive no credit for a blank and will probably receive some credit if you write something in answer to an essay question. If you guess a letter – say "B" for a multiple-choice question – you may have guessed right. If you leave a blank as an answer to a multiple-choice question, the examiners may respect your feelings but it will not add a point to your score. Some exams may penalize you for wrong answers, so in such cases *only*, you may not want to guess unless you have some basis for your answer.

7) Suggestions
   a. Objective-type questions
      1. Examine the question booklet for proper sequence of pages and questions
      2. Read all instructions carefully
      3. Skip any question which seems too difficult; return to it after all other questions have been answered
      4. Apportion your time properly; do not spend too much time on any single question or group of questions
      5. Note and underline key words – *all, most, fewest, least, best, worst, same, opposite,* etc.
      6. Pay particular attention to negatives
      7. Note unusual option, e.g., unduly long, short, complex, different or similar in content to the body of the question
      8. Observe the use of "hedging" words – *probably, may, most likely,* etc.
      9. Make sure that your answer is put next to the same number as the question
      10. Do not second-guess unless you have good reason to believe the second answer is definitely more correct
      11. Cross out original answer if you decide another answer is more accurate; do not erase until you are ready to hand your paper in
      12. Answer all questions; guess unless instructed otherwise
      13. Leave time for review

   b. Essay questions
      1. Read each question carefully
      2. Determine exactly what is wanted. Underline key words or phrases.
      3. Decide on outline or paragraph answer
      4. Include many different points and elements unless asked to develop any one or two points or elements
      5. Show impartiality by giving pros and cons unless directed to select one side only
      6. Make and write down any assumptions you find necessary to answer the questions
      7. Watch your English, grammar, punctuation and choice of words
      8. Time your answers; don't crowd material

8) Answering the essay question

Most essay questions can be answered by framing the specific response around several key words or ideas. Here are a few such key words or ideas:

M's: manpower, materials, methods, money, management
P's: purpose, program, policy, plan, procedure, practice, problems, pitfalls, personnel, public relations
a. Six basic steps in handling problems:
   1. Preliminary plan and background development
   2. Collect information, data and facts
   3. Analyze and interpret information, data and facts
   4. Analyze and develop solutions as well as make recommendations

5. Prepare report and sell recommendations
6. Install recommendations and follow up effectiveness

b. Pitfalls to avoid
1. *Taking things for granted* – A statement of the situation does not necessarily imply that each of the elements is necessarily true; for example, a complaint may be invalid and biased so that all that can be taken for granted is that a complaint has been registered
2. *Considering only one side of a situation* – Wherever possible, indicate several alternatives and then point out the reasons you selected the best one
3. *Failing to indicate follow up* – Whenever your answer indicates action on your part, make certain that you will take proper follow-up action to see how successful your recommendations, procedures or actions turn out to be
4. *Taking too long in answering any single question* – Remember to time your answers properly

EXAMINATION SECTION

EXAMINATION SECTION
TEST 1

DIRECTIONS: Each question or incomplete statement is followed by several suggested answers or completions. Select the one that BEST answers the question or completes the statement. *PRINT THE LETTER OF THE CORRECT ANSWER IN THE SPACE AT THE RIGHT.*

1. Of the following, the one LEAST recommended for routine control of "athlete's foot" is to
   A. dry the feet carefully after bathing
   B. dust the feet with medicated powder
   C. change socks daily
   D. apply gentian violet to the feet before retiring

1.____

2. A skin disorder caused by a fungus infection is
   A. athlete's foot   B. impetigo   C. boils   D. eczema

2.____

3. All of the following statements concerning the eye are correct EXCEPT:
   A. The tough, outer layer of the white of the eye is the sclera.
   B. The crystalline lens lies behind the pupil opening in the iris.
   C. The choroid layer of tissue surrounds and protects the retina.
   D. The rods are found in the retina.

3.____

4. Of the following, the INCORRECT association is:
   A. Ciliary muscles – control the shape of the lens of the eye
   B. Lacrimal gland – secretion of a saline solution
   C. Fovea centralis – region of poorest visual acuity
   D. Cones – cells sensitive to light

4.____

5. When reading a book, a student should be told to do all of the following EXCEPT to
   A. use a shaded light globe
   B. sit facing the light
   C. occasionally shift the eyes toward a distant object
   D. have the pages of the book clear of shadows

5.____

6. In assuming the crouch start in track, the sprinter brings all of the following muscle groups into action EXCEPT the
   A. flexor muscles of the shoulder joint
   B. extensor muscles of the spine
   C. flexor muscles of the knee
   D. extensor muscles of the hip

6.____

7. In chinning the bar, LEAST use is made of the _____ muscle:
   A. biceps   B. triceps
   C. pectorals   D. rectus abdominis

7.____

8. When the elbow joint is in the flexed position during a "pull-up," the forearm is in a _____ position.   8.____
   A. pronated   B. supinated   C. extended   D. abducted

9. All of the following muscle groups are in concentric contraction when pushing up from the floor to a front leaning rest EXCEPT the   9.____
   A. shoulder girdle abductors   B. shoulder joint flexors
   C. elbow joint extensors   D. wrist joint extensors

10. When a muscle contracts without changing its length, it is considered to be a(n) _____ contraction.   10.____
    A. isometric   B. isotonic   C. eccentric   D. concentric

11. Of the following exercises, the one BEST for strengthening and increasing the tone of the abdominal muscles is: 11.____
    A. Sit-ups from a lying position
    B. Trunk bending and stretching in the standing position
    C. Push-ups from a hand-support position
    D. The jumping jack

12. All of the following concerning the standing posture are correct EXCEPT that the   12.____
    A. knees should be extended but not stiff
    B. chest should be elevated but not puffed out
    C. hips should be drawn back slightly but not protruding
    D. head should be held high but not back

13. All of the following associations of body joint and use are correct EXCEPT: 13.____
    A. Ball and socket – freedom of motion
    B. Immovable – protection
    C. Hinge – power
    D. Gliding – slight rotation in two directions

14. In the Foster Test of Physical Efficiency, all of the following are noted EXCEPT the   14.____
    A. reclining pulse rate
    B. standing pulse rate
    C. increase in pulse rate immediately after exercise
    D. return of pulse rate after exercise

15. Of the following, the test which does NOT test cardiovascular efficiency is the _____ test.   15.____
    A. Barringer   B. Crampton   C. Sargent   D. Schneider

16. Of the following associations, the INCORRECT one is: 16.____
    A. Farsightedness – hyperopia   B. Nearsightedness – myopia
    C. Cross-eyed condition – astigmatism   D. Normal condition - emmetropia

17. Fluoridation of drinking water 　　　　　　　　　　　　　　　17.____
    A. can be used as a substitute for keeping teeth clean
    B. entails the elimination of the periodic care of teeth by the dentist
    C. allows for a reduction of intake of minerals in the daily balanced diet
    D. benefits to a greater degree children who drink it all their lives than adults
       who drink it in their post-teen years

18. In regard to proper cleaning of the surfaces of the teeth, of the following, 　18.____
    the MOST significant is the
    A. type of dentifrice
    B. timing of the process
    C. rinsing of the mouth on arising in the morning and retiring at night
    D. associated care of the gums

19. All of the following are membranes covering the brain EXCEPT the 　　　19.____
    A. dura mater 　　　B. peritoneum 　　C. pia mater 　　D. arachnoid

20. In regard to postural defects, the INCORRECT association is: 　　　　　20.____
    A. Torticollis – wry neck 　　　　　　　B. Kyphosis – round shoulders
    C. Lordosis – flat back 　　　　　　　　D. Scoliosis – abnormal spinal curve

21. All of the following associations are correct EXCEPT: 　　　　　　　　21.____
    A. Middle ear bones – smallest bones in the body
    B. Femur – strongest and heaviest bone in the body
    C. Patella – smallest uncalcified cartilage bone in the body
    D. Hip bone – broadest bone in the body

22. Of the following constituents of whole blood, the specific one instrumental 　22.____
    in starting the blood-clotting process is the
    A. white blood cells 　　　　　　　　　B. plasma
    C. platelets 　　　　　　　　　　　　　D. red blood cells

23. A condition caused by a deficient oxygenation of the blood is associated 　　23.____
    with the symptom of
    A. cheilosis 　　　　B. hematin 　　　C. cyanosis 　　　D. hypopnea

24. The presence of adrenalin in the blood does NOT 　　　　　　　　　　24.____
    A. make the heart beat faster
    B. raise the blood pressure
    C. enable the liver to provide extra sugar to the blood
    D. increase the clotting time of the blood

25. All of the following associations are correct EXCEPT: 　　　　　　　　25.____
    A. Anacusia – unconsciousness
    B. Analgesia – insensibility to pain
    C. Anesthesia – loss of sensation
    D. Anaphylaxis – sensitiveness to a protein

26. The germs which MOST often cause leaky heart valves are those present in
    A. scarlet fever and pneumonia   B. mumps and malaria
    C. meningitis and influenza   D. neuritis and measles

26.____

27. The HEAF test has contributed greatly in disclosing cases of
    A. diabetes   B. tuberculosis C. scarlet fever D. diphtheria

27.____

28. The three muscles that form the hamstring muscles are the
    A. gluteus maximus, pectineus, and tensor
    B. Sartorius, rectus femoris, and iliacus
    C. psoas, iliacus, and biceps femoris
    D. biceps femoris, semitendinosus, and semimembranosus

28.____

29. In the athlete, the process of "warming up" does all of the following EXCEPT to
    A. prepare his neuromuscular coordinating system for the impending task
    B. heighten his kinesthetic senses
    C. facilitate the biochemical reactions supplying energy for muscular contractions
    D. decrease tissue elasticity so that liability to injury is lessened

29.____

30. Of the following types of cerebral palsy, most cases fall into the _____ group.
    A. ataxic   B. rigidity   C. spastic   D. tremor

30.____

31. Heartburn is a(n)
    A. symptom of heart disease
    B. chemical disturbance in the stomach
    C. inflammation of the lining of the heart
    D. disturbance associated with the outer covering of the lungs

31.____

32. In regard to the planning of a physical activities program for students with cardiopathic conditions, it is INCORRECT to state that
    A. all cardiac students should be assigned to a restricted program
    B. a tolerance level for physical exercise for each participant must be established
    C. the program should have medical approval before it is administered
    D. the strenuousness of the activity for this type of student is determined by how vigorously and how long it is performed rather than by its type

32.____

33. The type of blood that can usually be given to any person needing a transfusion because it contains no agglutinogen is
    A. O   B. AB   C. B   D. A

33.____

34. All of the following statements concerning immunity are correct EXCEPT: 34.____
    A. Gamma globulin is an example of passive immunity.
    B. A vaccine is a serum which may contain weakened or dead germs.
    C. A substance that causes an individual to make his own antibodies is a toxoid.
    D. Temporary immunity is obtained by inducing the body to produce its own protection against a disease.

35. All of the following associations are correct EXCEPT: 35.____
    A. Agglutinins – antibodies causing certain elements to adhere to one another
    B. Precipitins – agent which counteracts the action of bacteria in the body
    C. Lysins – cell-dissolving substance
    D. Antigens – substance which stimulates the production of antibodies

36. All of the following associations are correct EXCEPT: 36.____
    A. Bronchitis – pertussis
    B. Hives – urticarial
    C. Lice – pediculosis
    D. Pink eye – acute contagious conjunctivitis

37. All of the following concerning diabetes are correct EXCEPT that it   37.____
    A. may be cured through diet and drug therapy
    B. seems to involve a hereditary factor
    C. is primarily a disease of middle and old age rather than of youth
    D. appears when the body tissues can neither use nor store sugar

38. All of the following are caused by thyroid gland malfunction EXCEPT   38.____
    A. acromegaly   B. myxedema   C. goiter   D. cretinism

39. All of the following are diseases of the alimentary tract EXCEPT   39.____
    A. typhus fever   B. hookworm   C. typhoid fever   D. cholera

40. Of the following diseases, the ones which tend to occur more frequently in the male rather than the female are   40.____
    A. tuberculosis and diabetes   B. goiter and impetigo
    C. color blindness and hemophilia   D. stomach ulcers and leukemia

41. In determining good walking posture, all of the following are correct EXCEPT having the   41.____
    A. heel make the first contact for each step
    B. arm swing controlled within a relatively small arc
    C. balance maintained over the body base with flexion at the hips and hyperextension in the lower back
    D. big toe at the origin of the push-off at each step

42. In determining good standing posture, of the following, the parts of the body that should be situated one above the other when viewed from the side are:
    A. Ear lobe, point of shoulder, hip joint, rear of patella
    B. Posterior end of jaw bone, crest of hip, back of knee
    C. Highest point of the ear, outer end of the clavicle, crest of the hip bone
    D. Nape of the neck, upper end of the femur, upper and lower ends of the fibula

42.____

43. Of the following, the BEST exercise to correct the condition of kyphosis is
    A. performing the jumping jack exercise
    B. flinging the arms vigorously sideward
    C. clasping the hands behind the body and stretching them downward past the hip area
    D. sitting with the spine pressed against the wall

43.____

44. The metatarsal arch exists
    A. for maintaining the height of the other arch of the foot
    B. only in non-weight-bearing positions
    C. for function of shock absorption
    D. primarily as a means of body support

44.____

45. Of the following, the BEST exercise to correct the condition of visceral ptosis is
    A. leg raising from a supine body position
    B. arching the back
    C. performing "sit-ups"
    D. bicycling

45.____

46. The esophagus is between the
    A. pharynx and the stomach
    B. epiglottis and the gullet
    C. larynx and the bronchus
    D. trachea and pylorus

46.____

47. The PRIMARY purpose of the Eustachian tube is to
    A. support the tympanic membrane
    B. aid the body in maintaining its equilibrium
    C. contain the semi-circular canals
    D. allow for the equalization of air pressure in the middle ear

47.____

48. Of the following, the exercise BEST suited to the development of the latissimus dorsi muscles is
    A. leg raising from the standing position
    B. chinning on the horizontal bar
    C. performing push-ups from the floor
    D. standing barbell presses

48.____

49. All of the following are important in tooth development EXCEPT vitamin
    A. A   B. C   C. B   D. D

49.____

50. All of the following concerning amino acids are correct EXCEPT: 50.____
    A. All amino acids contain carbon, hydrogen, oxygen, and nitrogen.
    B. Excess amino acids are stored in the involuntary musculature of the body.
    C. Proteins are made up of amino acids.
    D. Amino acids play an important role in maintaining both natural and acquired resistance to infection.

KEY (CORRECT ANSWERS)

1.	D	11.	A	21.	C	31.	B	41.	C
2.	A	12.	D	22.	C	32.	A	42.	A
3.	C	13.	D	23.	C	33.	A	43.	C
4.	C	14.	A	24.	D	34.	D	44.	B
5.	B	15.	C	25.	A	35.	B	45.	C
6.	B	16.	C	26.	A	36.	A	46.	A
7.	D	17.	D	27.	B	37.	A	47.	D
8.	A	18.	B	28.	D	38.	A	48.	B
9.	D	19.	B	29.	D	39.	A	49.	C
10.	A	20.	C	30.	C	40.	C	50.	B

TEST 2

DIRECTIONS: Each question or incomplete statement is followed by several suggested answers or completions. Select the one that BEST answers the question or completes the statement. *PRINT THE LETTER OF THE CORRECT ANSWER IN THE SPACE AT THE RIGHT.*

1. It is INCORRECT to state that cholesterol
   A. metabolism is related to atherosclerosis
   B. is a normal and essential constituent of human tissue
   C. levels in the blood are related to intake of animal fats
   D. levels in the blood are lowered b intake of saturated fats

   1.____

2. All of the following associations concerning milk are correct EXCEPT:
   A. Pasteurization – destruction of the common pathogens found in milk
   B. Homogenization – process of emulsifying milk
   C. Irradiation – sterilization of raw milk
   D. Centrifugalization – separation of cream from the milk

   2.____

3. No amount of vitamin D will serve to promote normal bone development unless the diet includes in adequate quantities
   A. calcium and phosphorus   B. sodium and sulfur
   C. iron and magnesium   D. potassium and carbon

   3.____

4. Of all of the following, the CORRECT statement is:
   A. Baby teeth need very little care because they will soon fall out.
   B. Reduction of starches and sweets in the diet generally helps maintain a healthy tooth.
   C. The use of tooth powders is sure to make a person's gums firm.
   D. The best way to brush the teeth is sideways.

   4.____

5. All of the following associations concerning teeth are correct EXCEPT:
   A. Dentine – bulk of the tooth
   B. Enamel – covering of the crown
   C. Periodontal membrane – pulp chamber
   D. Cementum – covering of the root

   5.____

6. Delayed dentition is usually due to
   A. long-standing caries in baby teeth
   B. thumbsucking
   C. rickets
   D. dental impaction

   6.____

7. There is evidence that all of the following disorders of the skin are caused by a virus infection EXCEPT
   A. common warts   B. shingles   C. moles   D. cold sores

   7.____

8. The SAFEST method of acquiring a suntan is the one in which   8.____
   A. a preparation is applied to provide a protective covering during the
      exposure time
   B. gradual exposure allows the skin to build natural resistance by increased
      pigmentation and thickening for an even tan
   C. exposure of the skin is started with reflected rays from water rather than
      from morning rays of direct sunlight
   D. skin is exposed to noon-day rays

9. In order to avoid eye fatigue during the viewing of a television program, the   9.____
   lighting arrangement in the room should provide light that
   A. is reflected on the screen
   B. brings about subdued general illumination of the room
   C. provides sharp contrast between the television screen and the
      surrounding area
   D. is located in the line of vision toward the screen

10. All of the following are correct reasons as to why it is necessary to maintain   10.____
    good posture when reading a book EXCEPT:
    A. Reading with the head bent forward strains the neck muscles.
    B. Viewing print at a sharp angle strains the eye muscles in their effort to
       focus.
    C. Studying a page in a book while lying down distorts the image on the
       page.
    D. Interpreting the printed page while sitting in a slouched position results in
       eye inflammation.

11. The INCORRECT association is: 11.____
    A. Cornea – transparent part of the outer layer of the eye
    B. Lens – part of the eye where light first enters to be focused on the retina
    C. Iris – muscle which control the size of the pupil
    D. Sclera – hard protective outer layer of the eye

12. Binocular vision is MOST important in   12.____
    A. forming impressions of depth
    B. providing a clear image of item on which eyes are focused
    C. reducing strain in each of the eyes
    D. intensifying receipt of light rays on the retina

13. All of the following are associated with the vitamin B complex EXCEPT   13.____
    A. riboflavin   B. folic acid
    C. ascorbic acid   D. nicotinic acid

14. The INCORRECT association is: 14.____
    A. Vitamin A – carotene   B. Thiamine – beriberi
    C. Riboflavin – pellagra   D. Vitamin C - gingivitis

15. The part of the small intestine that begins at the stomach is the   15.____
    A. jejunum   B. pylorus   C. ileum   D. duodenum

16. Lipase, which is necessary for the digestion of fats, is manufactured by the   16.____
    A. stomach   B. liver   C. pancreas   D. small intestine

17. A student suffering a loss of memory and the inability to speak as a result   17.____
    of a serious head injury would MOST likely have the _____ of the central
    nervous system damaged.
    A. cerebrum   B. medulla   C. spinal cord   D. cerebellum

18. An individual caught in a lightning storm has available the following shelters: 18.____
    I.   A large unprotected building
    II. A building which is protected against lightning
    III. A small unprotected building
    IV. A large metal or metal frame building

    The MOST logical, sequential order to use in his seeking shelter is:
    A. IV, II, I, III   B. II, I, IV, III   C. I, II, III, IV   D. IV, I, II, III

19. Food calories are   19.____
    A. units that measure fuel value   B. food nutrients
    C. fattening foods   D. the energy in foods

20. Iron is extremely important for   20.____
    A. repairing body tissue
    B. carrying oxygen to various parts of the body
    C. providing nourishment to nerve tissue
    D. bringing waste materials to the liver

21. All of the following statements are correct EXCEPT: 21.____
    A. The lack of iodine in the diet can cause goiter.
    B. The majority of all digested food is absorbed in the small intestine.
    C. A dietary deficiency of vitamin C can cause scurvy.
    D. Pepsin is the enzyme which helps digest fats.

22. The INCORRECT association of nutrient and food is: 22.____
    A. Protein –lean meats
    B. Carbohydrates – eggs
    C. Fats – butter
    D. Mineral salts – green leafy vegetables

23. All of the following associations of disease, cause, and symptom are   23.____
    correct EXCEPT:
    A. Chickenpox – virus – mild fever
    B. Malaria – protozoan – chills followed by high fever and sweating
    C. Osteomyelitis – bacteria – muscle spasms
    D. Tetanus – rickettsia – low temperature

24. All of the following associations are correct EXCEPT: 24.____
    A. Blepharitis – inflammation of the eyelids
    B. Chalazion – tumor of the eyelid
    C. Hordeolum – infection of the eyelid near a hair follicle
    D. Otitis media – cyst on the cornea

25. Of the following, the spleen is MOST closely related to the   25.____
    A. storage of red blood corpuscles   B. production of bile
    C. basal metabolism   D. digestion of fats

26. The epidermis contains   26.____
    A. blood vessels   B. small nerve endings
    C. adipose tissue   D. subcutaneous tissue

27. The duct of an oil gland usually empties into the   27.____
    A. blood vessel   B. hair follicle
    C. sweat pore   D. hair papilla

28. Of the following, the endocrine gland MOST closely associated with   28.____
    adulthood is the
    A. gonad   B. pineal   C. thymus   D. pituitary

29. All of the following associations are correct EXCEPT: 29.____
    A. Eustachian tube – middle ear
    B. Semi-circular canals – inner ear
    C. Auditory canal – outer ear
    D. Tympanic membrane – between the middle ear and the inner ear

30. All of the following statements are correct EXCEPT: 30.____
    A. Nerves reach into the interior of bones through the Haversian canals.
    B. The periosteum covers the surface of nearly all parts of the bone.
    C. Bone marrow consists mainly of minerals and proteins.
    D. The bone cells, or osteoblasts, are associated with the construction and
       repair of bones.

31. All of the following concerning leukocytes are correct EXCEPT that they   31.____
    A. are the source of gamma globulin
    B. have ameboid movement
    C. are found only in the blood of the body
    D. vary in number according to food intake and exercise

32. The disease characterized by defective ossification of the bones and the   32.____
    development of various bone deformation is
    A. arthritis   B. rickets   C. apoplexy   D. clubfoot

33. All of the following associations of disease and usual site of infection are   33.____
    correct EXCEPT:
    A. Botulism – nervous system   B. Cystitis – urinary bladder
    C. Diphtheria – throat   D. Rabies – bloodstream and lymph

34. In mumps, the gland affected is the 34._____
    A. lacrimal   B. parathyroid   C. parotid   D. pineal

35. All of the following associations are correct EXCEPT: 35._____
    A. Lysis – gradual decline in the manifestations of a disease
    B. Syndrome – a group of symptoms which characterize a disease
    C. Prognosis – prediction of the duration, course, and termination of a disease
    D. Precipitin – an infectious condition which develops into a contagious disease

36. All of the following associations are correct EXCEPT: 36._____
    A. Placebo – medicine given for the purpose of pleasing or humoring a patient
    B. Trauma – a form of injury
    C. Prolapse – falling down of an organ from its normal position
    D. Endemic – medication administered orally

37. Killed-virus vaccines 37._____
    A. multiply in the body
    B. can be taken by mouth or by inhalation
    C. must always be given by injection and in multiple doses
    D. have no expiration date for use since they do not become outdated

38. A person who has recovered from an attack of poliomyelitis is said to have _____ immunity. 38._____
    A. local   B. active acquired
    C. artificial   D. passive

39. All of the following diseases have been treated effectively by antibiotics EXCEPT: 39._____
    A. Tuberculosis and mastoid infection
    B. Scarlet fever and diphtheria
    C. Whooping cough and pneumonia
    D. Typhoid fever and thyroidism

40. All of the following statements are correct EXCEPT: 40._____
    A. The most powerful of the opiate drugs is heroin.
    B. A drug used as a painkiller is Benzedrine.
    C. A salt with a sedative effect on the nervous system is the bromide.
    D. The poisonous substance in tobacco is nicotine.

41. Of the following symptoms a student might display after receiving a blow to the head, the one MOST indicative of serious injury is 41._____
    A. pallor
    B. swelling
    C. dizziness
    D. inequality in size of pupils of the eyes

42. Good care of teeth does NOT include   42.____
    A. brushing the teeth immediately after eating
    B. increasing vitamin intake at mealtime
    C. rinsing the teeth forcefully with water right after meals
    D. removing adhering deposits and foreign matter trapped on and between the teeth and gums

43. Of the following, the INCORRECT association is: 43.____
    A. Dentition – eruption of teeth   B. Canines – cuspids
    C. Premolars – incisors   D. Third molars – wisdom teeth

44. Under normal conditions, drinking water which is artificially fluoridated in   44.____
the ratio of one part of fluorine to a million parts of water results in a(n)
    A. reduction of approximately 60% in the incidence of dental decay among children
    B. unsightly staining of children's teeth
    C. reduction of dental decay of equal effectiveness for children and adults
    D. neutralization of acids in the mouth

45. An inflammatory condition of the middle ear may be produced from infections   45.____
of the throat through the
    A. nose   B. Eustachian tube
    C. ear canal   D. tympanic membrane

46. The sweep frequency audiometer is NOT   46.____
    A. suitable for use in all school grades
    B. useful for those pupils who have a language handicap
    C. a machine that uses a comprehensive range of pitch tones
    D. employed to screen each child's hearing acuity individually

47. The term "ossicles" is MOST closely related to   47.____
    A. the brain   B. hearing   C. the ankle   D. the heart

48. When the two separate pictures of the eyes fuse properly to make one clear   48.____
image, it is considered satisfactory
    A. accommodation   B. refraction
    C. adaptation   D. binocular vision

49. All of the following help protect the eye EXCEPT the   49.____
    A. conjunctiva   B. lacrimal gland
    C. tarsal glands   D. choroid coating

50. Strabismus is a(n)   50.____
    A. condition which appears when the eyeball is too long from front to back
    B. condition that results when one pair of opposed rectus eye muscles is stronger than the other
    C. contagious disease of the cornea
    D. capacity of the crystalline lens of the eye

KEY (CORRECT ANSWERS)

1. D	11. B	21. D	31. C	41. D
2. C	12. A	22. B	32. B	42. B
3. A	13. C	23. D	33. D	43. C
4. B	14. C	24. D	34. C	44. A
5. C	15. D	25. A	35. D	45. B
6. C	16. C	26. B	36. D	46. D
7. C	17. A	27. B	37. C	47. B
8. B	18. A	28. A	38. B	48. D
9. B	19. A	29. D	39. D	49. D
10. D	20. B	30. C	40. B	50. B

EXAMINATION SECTION

TEST 1

DIRECTIONS: Each question or incomplete statement is followed by several suggested answers or completions. Select the one that BEST answers the question or completes the statement. *PRINT THE LETTER OF THE CORRECT ANSWER IN THE SPACE AT THE RIGHT.*

1. With respect to color blindness, it is an established fact that   1.____
   A. its cause is known by scientists
   B. more women than men are afflicted with this condition
   C. total color blindness is common
   D. victims of the most common type can see yellow and blue perfectly

2. A "pink eye" condition is MOST closely associated with   2.____
   A. glaucoma   B. opthalmia   C. conjunctivitis   D. sties

3. In regard to being overweight, it is CORRECT to state: 3.____
   A. High blood pressure is found twice as frequently in the overweight than in the underweight individual.
   B. Diabetes and arthritis are somewhat more common diseases of the underweight rather than the overweight.
   C. The underweight individuals are poorer surgical risks than the overweight individuals.
   D. A greater number of illnesses appear to attack the overweight rather than the underweight individuals.

4. If an individual really wants to lose weight, of the following, the MOST sensible   4.____
   way to do this is to
   A. decrease caloric intake   B. participate in active sports
   C. follow a diet of high protein intake   D. avoid animal fats

5. The liver is NOT associated with the   5.____
   A. storage of vitamins
   B. dispatching of sugars to the tissues for body fuel
   C. processing of iron for the blood system
   D. absorption of protein

6. All of the following associations of enzyme and digestive area are correct   6.____
   EXCEPT:
   A. Mouth – ptyalin   B. Small intestine – steapsin
   C. Stomach – rennin   D. Large intestine - pepsin

7. All of the following associations are correct EXCEPT: 7.____
   A. Ascorbic acid – scurvy   B. Vitamin D – rickets
   C. Vitamin A – night blindness   D. Vitamin E - beriberi

8. Of the following associations of food and the digestive juice that acts upon it,   8.____
    the INCORRECT one is:
    A. Cooked starch – salivary juice   B. Sugar – pancreatic juice
    C. Protein – gastric juice   D. Fat - bile

9. Of the following, the one that is NOT a salivary gland is the   9.____
    A. secretin   B. parotid   C. submaxillary   D. sublingual

10. A comparison of the heart rate and the blood pressure in the reclining   10.____
    position with corresponding values in the erect position is identified as the
    A. MacCurdy's Physical Capacity Index
    B. Roger's Athletic Index
    C. Crampton Blood Ptosis Test
    D. Oppenheimer's Scale

11. In regard to recently purchased iodine, nose drops, cough remedies, and   11.____
    other bottled medicines usually found in the home medicine cabinet, it is
    SAFEST to use the preparation if it
    A. has become cloudy
    B. is loosely corked
    C. was prescribed by the doctor for some previous illness
    D. had been kept in a cool, dark place

12. Of the following statements, the CORRECT one is: 12.____
    A. Suntan preparations enable an individual to stay in the sun longer with
        less risk of burning than without their use.
    B. Suntan lotions increase the speed of one's natural tanning mechanism.
    C. Suntan preparations shut out burning ultraviolet rays.
    D. The application of suntan preparations is more effective when used
        during exposure to direct midday hours of sun rather than used on hazy,
        lightly overcast days

13. Of the following, the SAFEST treatment for corns on toes is to   13.____
    A. apply a medicated moleskin plaster to the area
    B. wear well-fitted shoes
    C. cut off the mass of dead skin cells on the surface of the corn
    D. apply a corn remover

14. The PRIMARY purpose of melanin is to   14.____
    A. provide variation in the toughness of the skin
    B. prevent the more dangerous rays of the sun from damaging tissues
    C. convert surface skin on certain parts of the body into horny material
    D. dilate the blood vessels in the skin

15. All of the following associations are correct EXCEPT: 15.____
    A. Intracutaneous – within the layers of the skin
    B. Hypodermic – beneath the skin
    C. Subcutaneous – sweat glands over the entire skin surface
    D. Diaphoresis – perceptible perspiration

16. Children's bones do not break so easily as those of older persons because their bones   16.____
    A. are less flexible   B. do not carry as heavy a weight
    C. contain more cartilage   D. receive better nutritional foods

17. The inside of the shaft of a long bone is filled with   17.____
    A. yellow marrow   B. compact bony cells
    C. red blood cells   D. gelatinous tissue

18. All of the following statements are correct EXCEPT: 18.____
    A. There is more limited mobility of the big toe of the foot compared to that of the thumb on the hand.
    B. The foot bones are held together in such a way as to form springy lengthwise and crosswise arches.
    C. The much greater solidity of the big toe as compared to the fingers on the hand help the foot to support body weight.
    D. The phalanges of the foot are relatively more important than those of the hand and have a greater role in the functioning of the foot than those in the hand.

19. The condition that impairs the elasticity and function of the blood vessel walls and reduces the volume of blood that may pass through the afflicted arteries is   19.____
    A. hypertension   B. vascular occlusion
    C. high blood pressure   D. hardening of the arteries

20. The blood-clotting process in the body is started by the breaking-up of   20.____
    A. plasma   B. platelets
    C. white blood cells   D. red blood cells

21. The physician can actually see the arteries and veins at work when he   21.____
    A. measures the pressure of the walls of the blood vessels
    B. uses the ophthalmoscope in examining the eyes
    C. applies a fluoroscope in examining a patient
    D. uses the electrocardiograph

22. All of the following statements are correct EXCEPT: 22.____
    A. The figures used for the recording of blood pressure represent, in millimeters, the height of a column of mercury in the sphygmomanometer.
    B. In high blood pressure cases, progressive damage to the blood vessels takes place, whereas hypertension is limited to harder than normal work by the heart to pump the same amount of blood around to the tissues.
    C. In the recording of blood pressure, the larger figure represents the maximum pressure in the arteries with each heartbeat.
    D. The smaller figure in the recording of an individual's blood pressure registers the minimum pressure between heartbeats.

23. The red blood cells of the body are produced in the   23.____
   A. spongy area of the long bones, in the ribs, and in the vertebrae
   B. ends of the long bones and the spleen
   C. liver and the flat bones
   D. pancreas and the liver

24. Normally, upon exposure to air, blood clots form within _____ minutes.   24.____
   A. 30 seconds to two   B. three to ten
   C. ten to fifteen   D. fifteen to thirty

25. The CHIEF cause of heart disease in persons under 40 years of age is   25.____
   A. heredity   B. rheumatic fever
   C. obesity   D. elevated blood pressure

26. The accumulation of an oxygen debt by a normally healthy individual   26.____
   engaged in sport activity is related MOST directly to
   A. lack of endurance
   B. limited residual air
   C. strenuous exercise
   D. failure of the hemoglobin to combine with oxygen

27. All of the following are basic taste sensations EXCEPT _____ sensations.   27.____
   A. hot and cold   B. sweet   C. bitter   D. sour

28. A urine analysis does NOT test for the   28.____
   A. possibility of diabetes
   B. presence of albumin
   C. evidence of bladder or kidney inflammation
   D. growth of polyps in the urinary tract

29. The individual's esophagus is located between the   29.____
   A. pharynx and the stomach   B. mouth and the larynx
   C. small and large intestines   D. pharynx and the epiglottis

30. A physician's report indicate that a patient has injured the acromion. This   30.____
   injury is in the area of the
   A. ankle   B. knee
   C. elbow   D. shoulder blade

31. All of the following associations are correct EXCEPT: 31.____
   A. Bursa – cushion between the bones
   B. Cramp – an involuntary contraction of a muscle
   C. Strain – result of overuse of a muscle or group of muscles
   D. Tendon – stretchable tissue connecting bone to bone

32. Heparin is BEST known as a   32.____
   A. protein nutrient   B. antihistamine
   C. product of the pancreas   D. anticoagulant

33. All of the following associations are correct EXCEPT: 33.____
    A. Buccal cavity – mouth
    B. Glenoid cavity – arm socket
    C. Ventral cavity – intercostal spaces
    D. Medullary cavity – running the length of the shaft of a bone

34. The correct sitting posture does NOT include   34.____
    A. a flattened lumbar spine
    B. feet touching the floor
    C. placing the hips as far back in the seat as possible
    D. holding the head in the same position as when standing

35. All of the following associations of anatomic analysis and postural conditions   35.____
    are correct EXCEPT:
    A. Kyphosis – exaggerated convexity in the thoracic region of the vertebral column
    B. Scoliosis – lateral curvature in any region of the vertebral column
    C. Lordosis – exaggerated concavity in the lumbar region of the spine
    D. Kypho-lordosis – concavity in cervical and sacral regions of the spinal column

36. When moving heavy objects, do NOT   36.____
    A. bend at the hips and the knees
    B. push with the arms using the body and back as a brace
    C. lean against the object
    D. lower the body's center of gravity

37. The "rheumatoid factor" is   37.____
    A. a substance found in normal blood which reacts quickly to drugs
    B. the poor posture over several years which aggravates the bones and cartilage of the joints
    C. a protein substance found in the blood of rheumatoid arthritics
    D. the aches and pains that come with the passing years

38. Physical therapy helps the individual with arthritic joints by all of the   38.____
    following EXCEPT by
    A. preventing the joints from locking permanently
    B. improving the range of motion in the affected joint
    C. relieving inflammation of the joints
    D. helping avoid atrophy of the muscles

39. Of the following diseases, the one whose inoculation has the SHORTEST   39.____
    duration of effectiveness is
    A. measles   B. diphtheria
    C. smallpox   D. whooping cough

19

40. Normal increase in the size of a muscle is due to an increase in the   40.____
    A. number of muscle fibers
    B. thickness in the fibrous sheaths
    C. size of the individual muscle fibers
    D. capacity to convert lactic acid to glycogen

41. Pathogenic bacteria are characterized by their   41.____
    A. habitation in the digestive tract
    B. ability to produce vitamins
    C. presence in cheese and yeast molds
    D. ability to cause disease

42. All of the following concerning muscular contractions are correct EXCEPT: 42.____
    A. Uncoordinated muscular contractions involving an inconstant number of muscle groups are associated with convulsions.
    B. A sudden contraction of a muscle resulting from a single stimulus may be a simple muscular twitch.
    C. Tetanus is a sustained muscular contraction resulting from rapidly repeated stimuli.
    D. Muscle spasticity is incomplete muscular relaxation after repeated stimulation.

43. A physician's note explaining a student's absence mentions coryza. This indicates that the student had been suffering from   43.____
    A. St. Vitus Dance   B. a cold
    C. a kidney ailment   D. an eye infection

44. All of the following statements are true EXCEPT: 44.____
    A. As more energy is required by the body, the need for oxygen is increased.
    B. A cell will take only as much oxygen as it needs for use.
    C. Physical training increases the ability for oxygen consumption.
    D. Oxygen is stored in the living cell.

45. In subdividing the volumes of air respired by the normal adult, it is CORRECT to state that the   45.____
    A. tidal air is that amount of air that can be expelled after a normal expiration
    B. supplemental air is the amount of air that goes in and out with normal quiet breathing
    C. complemental air is the volume of air that can be taken in by the deepest inhalation after a normal inspiration
    D. residual air is the volume of air that can be expelled from deepest inspiration to fullest expiration

46. Rheumatic fever is a chronic disease that   46.____
    A. is both infectious and communicable
    B. can be prevented through the use of sulfonamide drugs
    C. is usually preceded by a hemolytic streptococcus infection
    D. is prevalent only among the malnourished

47. Diabetes mellitus is   47.____
    A. cured through the injection into the body of the appropriate dosage of
       insulin
    B. unrelated to weight but related to heredity
    C. primarily a problem of youth rather than middle and old age
    D. suspected when signs and symptoms in the individual include hunger,
       weakness, loss of appetite, excessive thirst, and frequent urination

48. In spinal meningitis, the   48.____
    A. nerves that carry messages to the spinal cord are injured
    B. nerves that carry messages to the muscles are damaged
    C. spinal cord is destroyed
    D. membrane around the brain is inflamed

49. All of the following are skin scratch tests for immunity or presence of disease   49.____
    EXCEPT the _____ test.
    A. Dick   B. Schick   C. Holmgren   D. Tuberculin

50. A virus is the causative agent for all of the following EXCEPT   50.____
    A. cholera   B. yellow fever   C. mumps   D. rabies

_____

KEY (CORRECT ANSWERS)

1.	D	11.	D	21.	B	31.	D	41.	D
2.	C	12.	A	22.	B	32.	D	42.	D
3.	A	13.	B	23.	A	33.	C	43.	B
4.	A	14.	B	24.	B	34.	A	44.	D
5.	D	15.	C	25.	B	35.	D	45.	C
6.	D	16.	C	26.	C	36.	B	46.	C
7.	D	17.	A	27.	A	37.	C	47.	D
8.	B	18.	D	28.	D	38.	C	48.	D
9.	A	19.	D	29.	A	39.	A	49.	C
10.	C	20.	B	30.	D	40.	C	50.	A

_____

TEST 2

DIRECTIONS: Each question or incomplete statement is followed by several suggested answers or completions. Select the one that BEST answers the question or completes the statement. *PRINT THE LETTER OF THE CORRECT ANSWER IN THE SPACE AT THE RIGHT.*

1.   The incubation period for MOST childhood diseases is   1.____
      A. 12 - 72 hours
      B. 1½ - 3 weeks
      C. 2 – 4 days
      D. based only on the child's resistance

2.   A positive reaction to the Heaf test signifies that the individual   2.____
      A. is suffering from tuberculosis
      B. is allergic to the serum
      C. is immune to tuberculosis
      D. should have a chest x-ray for further diagnosis

3.   It is CORRECT to state that   3.____
      A. streptomycin does not kill tuberculosis germs, but exerts a suppressive
          action which holds the tubercle bacilli in check
      B. a change of climate is the best treatment for tuberculosis
      C. a positive reaction to a tuberculin test indicates the disease is in its active
          form
      D. the Bacillus-Calmetta-Guerin vaccine is universally regarded as an
          effective vaccine for the control of tuberculosis

4.   All of the following diseases are caused by the hypofunction of ductless glands   4.____
      EXCEPT
      A. acromegaly   B. myxedema
      C. tetany   D. Addison's disease

5.   Substances which determine the various blood types are found in the   5.____
      A. white corpuscles   B. platelets
      C. red corpuscles   D. plasma

6.   All of the following substances are needed in blood clotting EXCEPT   6.____
      A. fibrinogen   B. lymph   C. prothrombin   D. calcium

7.   All of the following associations are correct EXCEPT: 7.____
      A. Blood group O – universal donor
      B. Blood group AB – universal recipient
      C. Rh factor – agglutinin
      D. Coagulant - heparin

8. All of the following statements are true EXCEPT: 8.____
   A. A goiter is an enlargement of the thyroid gland
   B. The mechanism associated with the sense of balance is located in the middle ear.
   C. The unit of structure of the nervous system is the neuron.
   D. In leukemia there is usually a great increase of white blood corpuscles in proportion to red corpuscles.

9. The larynx is between the 9.____
   A. pharynx and the nasal passages   B. esophagus and the thyroid
   C. nose and the thyroid cartilage   D. trachea and the pharynx

10. All of the following associations of types of joints are correct EXCEPT: 10.____
    A. Ball and socket – hip   B. Gliding – toes
    C. Pivot – head and neck   D. Hinge – elbow

11. The eight small bones that form the wrist are called the 11.____
    A. carpals   B. metatarsals   C. tarsals   D. phalanges

12. All of the following associations are correct examples of anatomic body levers EXCEPT the 12.____
    A. head tipping forward and backward – first class lever
    B. forearm flexed b the brachialis and biceps – third class lever
    C. arm raised sideward and upward by the deltoid muscle – second class lever
    D. forearm extended by the triceps muscle – first class lever

13. The condition in which the ankles deviate inward, throwing a great portion of body weight on the plantar ligaments and causing the medial portion of the foot to contact the ground, is called 13.____
    A. pes planus   B. pes cavus
    C. talipes varus   D. talipes calcaneus

14. Of the following, the MOST important muscle in maintaining the longitudinal arch of the foot during weight bearing is the 14.____
    A. flexor halluces longus   B. flexor digitorum longus
    C. tibialis posterior   D. peroneus longus

15. An absence of nicotinic acid in the diet results in a(n) 15.____
    A. condition characterized by an enlargement of the thyroid gland
    B. condition identified as gastric hypoacidity
    C. inflammation and cracking of the lips and the corners of the mouth
    D. disease of the skin and digestive tract

16. Liver is valuable in one's diet because it contains large amounts of 16.____
    A. phosphorus   B. vitamin D   C. iron   D. calcium

17. All of the following enzymes aid in the digestion of proteins EXCEPT 17.____
    A. ptyalin   B. pepsin   C. rennin   D. trypsin

18. Minerals in the daily diet are caused by the body to   18._____
    A. balance high calorific foods   B. provide body heat and energy
    C. stimulate and increase the appetite   D. regulate body processes

19. The pair of diseases that result from diet deficiencies is   19._____
    A. pellagra and hookworm   B. scurvy and botulism
    C. rickets and cheilosis   D. tularemia and typhoid

20. In a metabolism test,   20._____
    A. a graph is made of the patient's heart action
    B. the red and white corpuscles in a patient's blood are counted
    C. both the otoscope and the opthalmoscope are employed
    D. the amount of oxygen inhaled for a given period of time is determined

21. The swelling associated with a wrenched joint is caused by   21._____
    A. an unusual flow of synovial fluid
    B. decreased elasticity of the tendons
    C. poor muscle tone
    D. the effect of the wrench on the blood vessels

22. When a dislocation occurs, there is   22._____
    A. a bone out of place at a joint
    B. always a surface wound to be treated
    C. seldom, if any, pain
    D. less deformity than when a joint is sprained

23. A colles fracture is one which may affect the movement of the _____ joint.   23._____
    A. knee   B. shoulder   C. hip   D. wrist

24. In vision abnormalities, children are LEAST likely to be affected by   24._____
    A. strabisimus   B. presbyopia   C. hyperopia   D. myopia

25. Astigmatism is a condition which   25._____
    A. is characterized by an increase of tension in the eyeballs
    B. involves impairment of the eyes caused by a vitamin deficiency in the diet
    C. exists when the refracting surfaces of the eye are irregular
    D. is identified with eyeballs that are too short from front to back

26. The light-sensitive membrane forming the innermost coat of the eyeball   26._____
contains a pigment in the rods of the optic nerve which
    A. permits the automatic change in the convexity of the crystalline lens, thus insuring visual accommodation
    B. is capable of permitting light waves to pass obliquely from one transparent medium to another, thereby reducing the errors of refraction
    C. makes possible vision in dim light, thus reducing the incidence of twilight accidents
    D. stimulates the lachrymal glands, thus permitting the eyeball to be cleaned by means of tears

27. According to dental authorities, the brushing of teeth is MOST effective if done   27.____
    A. immediately after eating   B. in the morning and before retiring
    C. in the morning before breakfast   D. immediately before eating

28. The direct application of a 2% solution of sodium fluoride to the teeth of children at appropriate intervals   28.____
    A. is more effective in reducing the decay of teeth than artificially fluoridated water
    B. causes discoloration of teeth which decreases their decay-resistant qualities
    C. effectuates a condition in which decay among the treated teeth may be as much as 40% less than among the untreated
    D. is equally effective in preventing caries in adults

29. Children with a hearing loss of less than 20 decibels in either ear as detected in the pitch-tone test should be   29.____
    A. handled in school like any other normal group
    B. required to study lip reading
    C. fitted for a hearing aid
    D. allowed to move near any speaker or to select favorable seats in the classroom

30. The center of control for associative memory is in the   30.____
    A. medulla   B. pons   C. cerebrum   D. cerebellum

31. All of the following are correct EXCEPT: 31.____
    A. When taking an individual's pulse, count the pulse beats for one full minute, then check the rate by counting for another full minute.
    B. If there is any marked rise or drop in a patient's temperature, check the thermometer reading by takin the temperature again.
    C. When taking an individual's respiration rate, count for one full minute each rise of the chest.
    D. When taking the temperature at the armpit, the thermometer must be kept in position for five minutes before taking a reading.

32. Correct home nursing procedure for filling of a hot water bag includes all of the following EXCEPT: 32.____
    A. Testing the water so that it seems momentarily bearable to the clenched fist.
    B. Filling the bag one-third to one-half full.
    C. Expelling the air by placing the bag on a flat surface and screwing in the stopper when the water appears at the neck of the bag.
    D. Applying the bag to the affected part and reheating its contents when the skin ceases to be red.

33. In regard to the teeth, the   33.____
    A. bulk of the tooth is enamel
    B. root of the tooth is covered with cementum
    C. portion of the tooth above the gum is alveolus
    D. bony socket for the tooth is the dentin

34. All of the following are conditions which should be given immediate care by   34.____
    a dentist EXCEPT
    A. gingivitis   B. trench mouth
    C. malocclusion   D. pyorrhea

35. The SOUNDEST reason for following the dental rule "brush your teeth   35.____
    after every meal" is that
    A. this habit eliminates dental caries
    B. such a routine gets rid of tartar
    C. this procedure reduces halitosis
    D. since we end many meals with a sweet dessert, this habit helps rid the
       mouth of sugar

36. In general, eyeglasses are worn to correct all of the following EXCEPT   36.____
    A. sties   B. myopia
    C. hypermetropia   D. astigmatism

37. All of the following are common eye diseases EXCEPT   37.____
    A. pink eye   B. strabismus   C. glaucoma   D. trachoma

38. All of the following measure cardiovascular efficiency EXCEPT the _____   38.____
    test.
    A. Foster   B. Holmgren   C. Schneider   D. Crampton

39. The MOST reliable hearing test which can be administered by a nurse with   39.____
    some training in its use is the _____ test.
    A. watch-tick
    B. pure-tone (pitch-tone) audiometer
    C. phonograph audiometer
    D. whisper

40. The HEAF test determines the presence of   40.____
    A. measles   B. tuberculosis   C. diabetes   D. smallpox

41. When the feet are functioning as a support for the body, the MOST   41.____
    characteristic point about weak feet is
    A. their abducted position   B. the degree of rigidity
    C. the depressed transverse arches   D. the flexion of the toes

42. In attempting to correct a condition of weak feet, the individual should   42.____
    avoid
    A. toeing out when walking   B. walking on a balance beam
    C. "pencil writing" with the toes   D. gripping marbles with the toes

43. All of the following will affect the relation of the line of gravity to an individual's base of support EXCEPT carrying a
    A. heavy suitcase in the right hand
    B. tray in both hands in front of the chest
    C. basketball in a dribble position
    D. moderately heavy basket on the head

43.____

44. A condition in which a series of vertebrae remains constantly deviated from the normal spinal axis accompanied by a degree of rotation of the vertebrae is known as
    A. kypholordosis   B. structural scoliosis
    C. mobile scoliosis   D. functional scoliosis

44.____

45. The gland which has the GREATEST influence on the rate of oxygen consumption is the
    A. thyroid   B. pineal   C. adrenal   D. buccal

45.____

46. Training of the muscular system brings about all of the following EXCEPT an increase in the
    A. strength of the muscles   B. endurance of the muscles
    C. number of muscle fibers   D. size of the muscles

46.____

47. It is the belief of predominant authority that tonsils are
    A. lymphoid tissues which protect the body by collecting bacteria
    B. secreting glands
    C. centers of temperature control
    D. useless

47.____

48. A first-class lever is seen in action when the
    A. triceps extend the elbow   B. brachialis flexes the elbow
    C. biceps flex the elbow   D. deltoid abducts the arm

48.____

49. All of the following concerning joints are correct EXCEPT:
    A. The synovial fluid lubricates the joint.
    B. The capsule determines the degree of movement in the joint.
    C. Ligaments help hold the ends of the bones at the joint in place.
    D. Cartilage decreases friction between the two bones.

49.____

50. The MAIN sources of body heat are the
    A. lungs and pancreas   B. muscles and the liver
    C. skin and large intestines D. intestines and the stomach

50.____

KEY (CORRECT ANSWERS)

1.	B	11.	A	21.	A	31.	D	41.	A
2.	D	12.	C	22.	A	32.	D	42.	A
3.	A	13.	A	23.	D	33.	B	43.	D
4.	A	14.	C	24.	B	34.	C	44.	B
5.	C	15.	D	25.	C	35.	D	45.	A
6.	B	16.	C	26.	C	36.	A	46.	C
7.	D	17.	A	27.	A	37.	B	47.	A
8.	B	18.	D	28.	C	38.	B	48.	A
9.	D	19.	C	29.	D	39.	B	49.	B
10.	B	20.	D	30.	C	40.	B	50.	B

TEST 1

DIRECTIONS: Each question or incomplete statement is followed by several suggested answers or completions. Select the one that BEST answers the question or completes the statement. *PRINT THE LETTER OF THE CORRECT ANSWER IN THE SPACE AT THE RIGHT.*

1. All of the following are associated with movement of the femur at the hip joint EXCEPT:
   A. Flexion - outward rotation
   B. Inversion – supination
   C. Inward rotation – circumduction
   D. Extension - abduction

   1.____

2. Of the following, the one necessary for the formation of thyroxin, which controls the metabolic rate, is
   A. phosphorus
   B. sodium chloride
   C. iodine
   D. calcium

   2.____

3. Excluding the coronary circulation, the average time for the complete circulation of the blood through all the circuits of the adult human body is APPROXIMATELY
   A. 23 seconds
   B. 5 minutes
   C. 1 minute, 15 seconds
   D. 10 minutes

   3.____

4. All of the following associations are correct EXCEPT:
   A. Myocarditis – inflammation of the valves of the heart
   B. Pericarditis – inflammation of the sac enveloping the heart
   C. Endocarditis – inflammation of the lining membrane of the heart
   D. Aortitis – inflammation of the vessel leading out of the lower left chamber of the heart

   4.____

5. All of the following are directly associated with the heart beat EXCEPT the
   A. pacemaker
   B. semilunar valves
   C. right atrium
   D. bundle of His

   5.____

6. Of the following, the substance necessary for the clotting of blood is
   A. ptyalin
   B. prothrombin
   C. gastrin
   D. rennin

   6.____

7. Of the following, the ones which CANNOT be converted into heat or other forms of energy are
   A. fats
   B. proteins
   C. minerals
   D. carbohydrates

   7.____

8. Of the following reasons for recommending cod liver oil for growing children, the INCORRECT one is that it   8.____
   A. contains a vitamin which is a growth factor for the young
   B. aids digestion of other foods
   C. is an inexpensive source of vitamins A and D

9. Of the following suggestions for reducing weight, the one MOST likely to be given by doctors to their otherwise healthy patients is to   9.____
   A. omit all desserts and bread
   B. increase the protein intake, to omit duplication in starches at each meal, and to eat low calorie desserts
   C. omit potatoes, bread, and all desserts except fruit for the main meal
   D. follow a diet made up entirely of protein, fruit, and vegetables

10. As a rule, the one which has the LONGEST incubation period is   10.____
    A. chickenpox   B. diphtheria   C. scarlet fever   D. influenza

11. All of the following associations are correct EXCEPT: 11.____
    A. Parotid gland – mumps
    B. Adrenal gland – Addison's disease
    C. Parathyroid gland – acromegaly
    D. Pituitary gland - gigantism

12. Blood sugar is LOW   12.____
    A. in untreated diabetes mellitus
    B. during emotional stress
    C. after meals
    D. during severe and prolonged muscular exertion

13. All of the following statements are correct EXCEPT: 13.____
    A. A group of symptoms that occur together and characterize a disease is a syndrome.
    B. A turning point in a disease in which a decisive change one way or another is impending is known as the crisis.
    C. The prognosis of a disease is a prediction of the disease's duration, course, and termination.
    D. A sequela of a disease is a chronic condition of the disease that persists throughout its course.

14. Active immunity may be acquired in all of the following ways EXCEPT by   14.____
    A. injections of dead bacteria or their toxins
    B. recovery from certain diseases
    C. injections of phagocytes into the bloodstream
    D. the cumulative effect of several slight exposures to certain diseases

15. All of the following associations are correct EXCEPT: 15._____
    A. Dynamometer – measuring muscle strength
    B. Manometer – measures strength of hand grip
    C. Anthropometry – measurement of the body or its various parts
    D. Ergometer – calculates work performed by a muscle or group of muscles over a specified time

16. The substances which are NOT necessary for building new tissues are   16._____
    A. water   B. carbohydrates
    C. proteins   D. minerals

17. A nutrient functions in any or all of the following ways EXCEPT   17._____
    A. furnish energy
    B. provide materials for building or maintenance of body tissues
    C. help regulate body processes
    D. purify the blood

18. It is MOST important to see that reducing diets of adolescents do NOT lack   18._____
    A. fats   B. proteins
    C. carbohydrates   D. simple sugars

19. The CHIEF value of cellulose in the diet is that it   19._____
    A. is more soluble than starch
    B. gives bulk to the intestinal residues
    C. is easily digested
    D. provides an essential amino acid

20. It is CORRECT to state that enzymes   20._____
    A. are used up in chemical reactions of foods
    B. retard the process of breaking down of foods
    C. work only in acid surroundings
    D. are specific in their action

21. All of the following are important functions of fat EXCEPT that it   21._____
    A. supports and protects organs
    B. prevents the loss of heat from the body surface
    C. is used in the building and repairing of tissues
    D. serves as a reserve supply of fuel

22. All of the following concerning cheese made from whole milk are correct EXCEPT that it   22._____
    A. preserves its milk nutrients for longer periods than the liquid itself
    B. is readily digested provided it is eaten slowly and in moderation
    C. loses its fat value when cooked
    D. is a source of riboflavin

23. The sugar which can be used by the body without having to be broken down into simpler sugars is   23._____
    A. lactose   B. glucose   C. maltose   D. sucrose

24. The cells which have the property of engulfing and digesting foreign particles   24.____
    harmful to the body are called
    A. osteocytes   B. phagocytes   C. mast   D. plasma

25. The INCORRECT association of covering and tissue is: 25.____
    A. Periosteum – bone   B. Perimysium – muscle
    C. Peritoneum – heart   D. Perichondrium - cartilage

26. An acquired reduction in size of an organ which has previously reached   26.____
    mature size is called
    A. hyperothrophy   B. atrophy   C. necrosis   D. calcification

27. All of the following associations are correct EXCEPT: 27.____
    A. Myocardial – pertaining to the heart muscle
    B. Myoneural – pertaining to both muscle and nerve
    C. Myogenic – having origin in the muscle
    D. Myocytic – pertaining to muscular spasm

28. All of the following are concerned with the clotting of blood EXCEPT   28.____
    A. cholesterol   B. blood platelets
    C. vitamin K   D. prothrombin

29. Blood plays an important role in all of the following EXCEPT in the   29.____
    A. removal of waste products
    B. regulation of body temperature
    C. maintenance of water balance
    D. production of acidity of body fluids

30. Of the following, the gland MOST closely related to muscular efficiency   30.____
    is the
    A. adrenal   B. gonads   C. pituitary   D. thyroid

31. The INCORRECT association of gland and location is: 31.____
    A. Pineal – brain cavity
    B. Parotid – below and in front of the ear
    C. Sumaxillary – below each lower jaw
    D. Thymus – at the larynx

32. The LARGEST source of body heat is the _____ system.   32.____
    A. digestive   B. muscular   C. tegumentary   D. nervous

33. The three points of support of the longitudinal arch of the foot include all   33.____
    of the following EXCEPT the
    A. anterior head of the first metatarsal bone
    B. anterior head of the fifth metatarsal bone
    C. anterior head of the astragalus
    D. calcaneus

34. Long bone growth is at its maximum in the _____ period. 34._____
    A. adolescent　　　　　　　　B. pre-adolescent
    C. early childhood　　　　　　D. infancy

35. The acetabulum is the articular cup in a one which acts as a socket for the 35._____
    A. clavicle　　B. femur　　C. radius　　D. tibia

36. Of the following associations, the CORRECT one is: 36._____
    A. Second class lever – the forearm when it is being extended by the triceps muscle
    B. Third class lever – the foot when rising on the toes
    C. First class lever – the head tipping forward and backward
    D. Second class lever – the arm when it is raised sideward-upward by the deltoid muscle

37. The INCORRECT statement is: 37._____
    A. The heart of the adolescent is especially vulnerable to the stress of exercise.
    B. Exercise tolerance of children is usually higher than that of adults.
    C. Cardiac examinations have shown that the world's best athletic performers in the Olympics have hearts larger than normal.
    D. Participation in competitive athletics should be postponed pending complete recovery after infections.

38. Blood pressure is associated with all of the following EXCEPT the 38._____
    A. force of the heart beat
    B. elasticity of the walls of the blood vessels
    C. number of leucocytes present in the blood
    D. viscosity of the blood

39. In infancy _____ is(are) more rapid than in adulthood. 39._____
    A. the heart beat　　　　　　B. the oxidation processes
    C. the respiration rate　　　　D. all of the above

40. All of the following are correct principles relating to the muscular system EXCEPT: 40._____
    A. Muscles contract more rapidly following warm-up activities.
    B. Muscular strength is progressively developed by the repetition of exercises of the same intensity.
    C. Muscles contract more forcefully if they are first stretched, provided that they are not overstretched.
    D. A muscle must be loaded beyond its customary load if strength is to be increased.

41. Gradations in muscular contraction are related to 41._____
    A. variations in intensity of muscular contraction
    B. the number of fibers in the muscle which contract
    C. the circulation of blood within the muscle
    D. the manufacture of lactic acid in the muscle

42. In order to determine the basal metabolic rate of an individual, all of the following conditions must be included EXCEPT that the
    A. environment temperature must be comfortably warm
    B. test must be made from 12 to 18 hours after the last meal
    C. body must be in the waking state and at complete rest
    D. test should be preceded by a ten-minute period of vigorous exercise

42.____

43. Static and moving body postures are BEST judged on the basis of
    A. how well they meet the demands made upon them
    B. comparison with standardized charts
    C. muscular strength
    D. body flexibility

43.____

44. All of the following increase the efficiency of lifting heavy objects from the floor EXCEPT
    A. flexing the knees
    B. bending forward from the waist
    C. holding the object as close to the body as possible
    D. keeping the feet slightly separated both laterally and anteroposteriorly

44.____

45. All of the following associations are correct EXCEPT:
    A. Dorsal flexion – bending the foot at the ankle and elevating the front of the foot and toes
    B. Supination – turning the foot outward at its relation to the leg
    C. Plantar flexion – depressing the front of the foot and toes
    D. Adduction – turning the foot inward in its relation to the leg

45.____

46. All of the following concerning the Kraus-Weber Test for muscular fitness are correct EXCEPT:
    A. Failure on any one of the subtests classifies a child as a muscular-fitness failure.
    B. Flexibility in this test is measured by having the child bend forward slowly and touch his fingertips to the floor without bending his knees.
    C. The grip-strength test does not have much value since there is little relationship between grip strength and general body strength.
    D. The test measures large muscle groups of the upper and lower back, the abdominal wall and flexors of the hip joint.

46.____

47. Of the following, the one which is designed to reveal whether a child's growth is progressing properly in terms of his own body build is the
    A. Pryor Width-Weight Tables
    B. Wetzel Grid
    C. Quinby Weight Analysis Test
    D. Rogers Strength Index of Physical Fitness Index

47.____

48. The center of gravity of an individual of average build in an erect standing position is
    A. located in the pelvis in front of the upper part of the sacrum
    B. located at the articulation of the femur and the pelvis

48.____

C. located in the anterior wall of the pelvis
D. lower in men than in women because of anatomical structure

49. All of the following statements concerning lateral curvatures of the spine are correct EXCEPT:
    A. Some rotation of the vertebrae always accompanies lateral flexion of the spine.
    B. In a simple structural lateral curvature, the curve is confined to one region and there is no compensator curve.
    C. The shoulder on the side of a dorsal convexity is lower than the other shoulder.
    D. In a functional lateral curvature of the spine, the curve disappears when the individual suspends his body by hanging from the arms.

49.____

50. Vitamin A deficiency is associated with all of the following EXCEPT
    A. faulty development of the teeth
    B. impairment of vision in dim light
    C. impairment of epithelial tissue
    D. retardation in the development of bones

50.____

KEY (CORRECT ANSWERS)

1.	B	11.	C	21.	C	31.	D	41.	B
2.	C	12.	D	22.	C	32.	B	42.	D
3.	A	13.	D	23.	B	33.	C	43.	A
4.	A	14.	C	24.	B	34.	B	44.	B
5.	B	15.	B	25.	C	35.	B	45.	B
6.	B	16.	B	26.	B	36.	C	46.	C
7.	C	17.	D	27.	D	37.	A	47.	B
8.	B	18.	B	28.	A	38.	C	48.	A
9.	B	19.	B	29.	D	39.	D	49.	C
10.	A	20.	D	30.	A	40.	B	50.	D

TEST 2

DIRECTIONS: Each question or incomplete statement is followed by several suggested answers or completions. Select the one that BEST answers the question or completes the statement. *PRINT THE LETTER OF THE CORRECT ANSWER IN THE SPACE AT THE RIGHT.*

1. All of the following concerning a universal blood donor are correct EXCEPT that he   1.____
   A. is a person whose blood is of type O
   B. is one whose blood corpuscles are not agglutinated by the blood of anyone
   C. may give his blood to a person whose blood is type A or type B
   D. is the only type accepted for a blood bank

2. Dried blood plasma can be made available for an emergency transfusion by the addition of   2.____
   A. a saline solution
   B. an alkaline fluid
   C. blood cells
   D. sterile distilled water

3. All of the following are subjective symptoms EXCEPT a   3.____
   A. headache
   B. flushed face
   C. sore throat
   D. earache

4. When taking the wrist pulse rate, one should avoid   4.____
   A. taking the pulse with the thumb
   B. counting the pulse beats for 1 minute, then checking the rate by counting for another minute
   C. having the patient support his arm and hand in a relaxed position
   D. taking the pulses on the thumb side of the wrist between the tendon and the wrist bone

5. All of the following associations are correct EXCEPT: 5.____
   A. Etiology – science of the causes of diseases
   B. Sequela – abnormal consequence persisting after the recovery from a disease
   C. Prognosis – prediction of the duration, course, and termination of a disease
   D. Incubation – associated alterations of structure and functions during the course of a disease

6. All of the following diseases are caused by a virus EXCEPT   6.____
   A. diphtheria   B. herpes   C. mumps   D. chickenpox

7. All of the following destroy or inhibit microorganisms EXCEPT   7.____
   A. prophylactics   B. antiseptics   C. disinfectants   D. germicides

8. All of the following associations are correct EXCEPT:　　　　　　　8.____
   A. Smallpox – rubeola　　　　　B. German measles – rubella
   C. Mumps – infectious parotitis　D. chickenpox - varicella

9. Of the following, the one NOT related to the other three is　　　　9.____
   A. antidote　　　B. antibody　　C. antitoxin　　D. antigen

10. In regard to rheumatic fever, it is CORRECT to state that　　　　10.____
    A. it can be passed on from one person to another
    B. it is responsible for more heart trouble in children than any other cause
    C. once a child has had this disease, he is not liable to another attack
    D. there is a specific test for diagnosing the disease

11. Ringworm is caused by a microscopic　　　　　　　　　　　　11.____
    A. mold　　　　B. worm　　　C. yeast　　　D. virus

12. All of the following associations of suffixes found in technical terms on a　　12.____
    health record and meanings are correct EXCEPT:
    A. Osis – swelling　　　　B. Emia – blood
    C. Itis – inflammation　　D. Algia - pain

13. All of the following associations are correct EXCEPT:　　　　　13.____
    A. Active immunity – smallpox vaccination
    B. Passive immunity – diphtheria antitoxin
    C. Acquired immunity – resistance to another attack of measles
    D. Local immunity – resistance to a disease by a group of individuals within
       a limited area

14. All of the following statements are correct EXCEPT:　　　　　14.____
    A. The only carbohydrate found in the blood and used by the body is
       glucose.
    B. The liver is the great regulator of the blood sugar.
    C. The main storage house of excess carbohydrate stored in the body is the
       connective tissue.
    D. Glycogen is the term applied to the excess carbohydrate stored in the
       body.

15. All of the following are associated with the diffusion of digested foods EXCEPT　15.____
    A. arterioles　　　B. capillaries　　C. lymph　　　D. villi

16. All of the following statements are correct EXCEPT:　　　　　16.____
    A. More than half of the iron in the body is in the hemoglobin of the red blood
       cells.
    B. Iron deficient persons can absorb more iron from food than healthy
       persons.
    C. Iron is relatively high in foods of low moisture content.
    D. When the diet's supply of iron is in excess of body needs, it is stored in
       the liver for later use.

17. All of the following are associated with vitamin D EXCEPT   17.____
    A. ergosterol   B. sorbitol   C. calciferol   D. viosterol

18. The enzyme in the gastric juice that causes the curdling or coagulation of   18.____
    milk is
    A. renin   B. pepsin   C. rennin   D. lipase

19. Of the following, the one that is NOT associated with a lack of vitamins is   19.____
    A. beri-beri   B. zerophthalmia
    C. trachoma   D. night blindness

20. All of the following associations are correct EXCEPT: 20.____
    A. Folic acid – vitamin B   B. Tetany – parathyroids
    C. Trypsin – gastric juice   D. Insulin - pancreas

21. All of the following associations are correct EXCEPT: 21.____
    A. Vitamin E – antihemorrhagic
    B. Vitamin C – anti-scorbutic
    C. Vitamin B – anti-neuritic
    D. Nicotinic acid – pellagra preventive

22. All of the following forms of milk are comparable in food nutrients EXCEPT   22.____
    A. certified milk   B. evaporated milk
    C. buttermilk   D. homogenized milk

23. All of the following statements are correct EXCEPT: 23.____
    A. The presence of a sufficient quantity of fats in the diet does away with the
       necessity of using protein for fuel.
    B. Any considerable amount of fat in food eaten will slow down the digestion
       of the whole meal.
    C. The digestion of fats begins in the stomach.
    D. Layers of fat under the skin help to keep the body temperature constant.

24. All of the following are ductless glands EXCEPT the   24.____
    A. parotid   B. pineal   C. thymus   D. adrenals

25. Of the following, the tissue that has a capillary system is the   25.____
    A. dermis   B. hair
    C. nails   D. outer layer of skin

26. All of the following concerning a bursa are correct EXCEPT that   26.____
    A. it is a closed sac which contains a small amount of fluid
    B. its inner lining secretes fluid
    C. it prevents friction between muscles and underlying parts
    D. arthritis is caused by inflammation of the bursa

27. The body's CHIEF means of increasing heat production is by   27.____
    A. perspiring   B. dilating the blood vessels
    C. shivering   D. none of the above

28. With regard to nerve cells, the CORRECT statement is: 28.____
    A. They may be regenerated once they are destroyed in the body.
    B. They greatly increase in number after birth.
    C. They have a single axon and one or more dendrites.
    D. Messages may be transmitted either way between axons and dendrites.

29. The substance in the blood which plays a very important part in protecting   29.____
the body against infection is
    A. heparin   B. cholesterol   C. properdin   D. hematin

30. The grouping of types of human blood is based upon the type of   30.____
    A. red corpuscles   B. thrombocytes
    C. platelets   D. white corpuscles

31. The contractions of the heart cause all of the following EXCEPT   31.____
    A. the arterial blood to move via the aorta to all parts of the body
    B. the lymph to move through the lymph capilaries into larger lymph vessels
    C. the venous blood to go to the lungs for oxygen via the pulmonary arteries
    D. intermittent changes in the shape of the arteries

32. All of the following concerning the epidermis are correct EXCEPT that it   32.____
    A. contains nerve fibers
    B. contains blood cells
    C. constantly renews itself by creating new cells which push upward
    D. can become thicker after a long period of constant rubbing and pressure

33. A patient who has acne should be advised to   33.____
    A. wash his face thoroughly at least twice a day with a mild soap and warm
       water
    B. apply a cleansing cream when retiring at night
    C. use a skin ointment with an oily base at night and in the morning
    D. squeeze the pimple or blackhead and apply iodine

34. All of the following concerning the feet are correct EXCEPT: 34.____
    A. The height of the arch is an indication of the strength of the foot.
    B. Arch supports are temporary expedients for the relief of foot pain.
    C. Neglected, weak feet become flexible flat feet.
    D. Rigid flat feet show depressed arches when the weight is not borne on
       the feet.

35. All of the following are deformities of the foot EXCEPT   35.____
    A. calcaneus   B. talipes valgus
    C. equinus   D. genu valgum

36. The INCORRECT association is: 36.____
    A. Endomorph – soft, round, tendency to lay on fat
    B. Somatomorph – tall, athletic, broad-shouldered
    C. Ectomorph – linear, fragile, delicate
    D. Mesomorph – square, rugged, hard

37. All of the following are important components of the visual act proper EXCEPT   37.____
    A. convergence   B. interpretation
    C. accommodation   D. fusion

38. The condition of the eye in which the eyeball is too long anterioposteriorly is   38.____
known as
    A. ametropia   B. hypermetropia
    C. myopia   D. prebyopia

39. When the nurse tests students' vision by means of the Snellen chart, she   39.____
is testing the students'
    A. peripheral vision   B. distance acuity
    C. near acuity   D. depth perception

40. All of the following statements concerning protein are correct EXCEPT: 40.____
    A. Protein is a source of energy.
    B. Protein is required for tissue building and repair.
    C. Vegetable proteins are generally as satisfactory as meat proteins in
        meeting body requirements.
    D. Cheese contains important animal proteins.

41. Foods rich in calcium and protein are also the BEST sources of   41.____
    A. iodine   B. phosphorus   C. copper   D. fluorine

42. A lack of thiamine in the diet may cause   42.____
    A. inability to see in a dim light
    B. lesions around the nose and eyes
    C. malnourishment of the bones
    D. impaired functioning of the digestive and nervous system

43. The food which is acid-forming is   43.____
    A. fruits   B. vegetables   C. meat   D. nuts

44. The LEAST desirable method of preparing vegetables is by   44.____
    A. adding baking soda to preserve the color
    B. steaming
    C. boiling for a short time in a small amount of water
    D. baking

45. A low-calorie diet should NOT be low in _____ content.   45.____
    A. fat   B. fluid
    C. carbohydrate   D. protein

46. Skim milk is rich in all of the following EXCEPT   46.____
    A. calcium   B. riboflavin   C. vitamin A   D. protein

47. Food allergies are due to sensitization to a   47.____
    A. carbohydrate   B. fat   C. mineral   D. protein

48. With regard to nutrition, the CORRECT statement is: 48.____
    A. Malnutrition is found only in low-income families.
    B. Obesity is generally due to faulty glands.
    C. Nutrition is affected by rest, recreation, and general mental health.
    D. Adolescents should take additional vitamin preparations in order to ensure adequate vitamin intake.

49. In order to improve the muscular state of the nation, it would be desirable to 49.____
    do all of the following for our youth EXCEPT to
    A. encourage participation in daily calisthenics
    B. promote participation in swimming
    C. popularize soccer as a game for school children
    D. emphasize competitive sports

50. The Menninger Foundation and Clinic is known for its work in 50.____
    A. posture   B. nutrition
    C. mental health   D. cancer research

KEY (CORRECT ANSWERS)

1. D	11. A	21. A	31. B	41. B
2. D	12. A	22. C	32. B	42. D
3. B	13. D	23. C	33. A	43. C
4. A	14. C	24. A	34. A	44. A
5. D	15. A	25. A	35. D	45. D
6. A	16. B	26. D	36. B	46. C
7. A	17. B	27. C	37. B	47. D
8. A	18. C	28. C	38. C	48. C
9. A	19. C	29. C	39. B	49. D
10. B	20. C	30. A	40. C	50. C

EXAMINATION SECTION
TEST 1

DIRECTIONS: Each question or incomplete statement is followed by several suggested answers or completions. Select the one that BEST answers the question or completes the statement. *PRINT THE LETTER OF THE CORRECT ANSWER IN THE SPACE AT THE RIGHT.*

1. All of the following increase the efficiency of lifting heavy objects from the floor EXCEPT   1.____

    A. bending forward from the waist
    B. flexing the knees
    C. keeping the feet slightly separated both laterally and anterioposteriorly
    D. holding the object as close to the body as possible

2. In the exercise of "double leg lifting" while in a supine position, the abdominal muscles act as   2.____

    A. stabilizers   B. prime movers
    C. neutralizers   D. assistant movers

3. The vastus medialis and the popliteus are muscles primarily involved with movement of the   3.____

    A. elbow   B. knee   C. neck   D. hip

4. The strength of any group of muscles can be tested MOST accurately by means of a   4.____

    A. dynamometer   B. stadiometer
    C. spirometer   D. sphymomanometer

5. The CORRECT association is   5.____

    A. sartorius - chest   B. gastrocnemius - leg
    C. trapezius - foot   D. pectoralis minor - back

6. Exercises for those with chronic heart conditions should   6.____

    A. consist of isometrics
    B. be completely eliminated
    C. consist of simple, light movements
    D. be mildly competitive

7. Movement in the ankle is accomplished with the aid of a _____ joint.   7.____

    A. hinged   B. pivot
    C. gliding   D. ball and socket

8. The CORRECT association of suffix and meaning is   8.____

    A. ology - disease   B. itis - inflammation
    C. algia - blood   D. hemia - skin

9. The duodenum is part of the   9.____

    A. small intestine   B. stomach
    C. pancreas   D. large intestine

10. In lordosis, there is an exaggeration of the _____ curve.   10._____

    A. lumbar   B. sacral   C. cervical   D. dorsal

11. Diuresis is the   11._____

    A. presence of blood in urine
    B. involuntary passage of urine
    C. presence of infection in the bladder
    D. increase in the daily amounts of urine elimination

12. Psoriasis is a _____ disorder.   12._____

    A. postural   B. skin   C. heart   D. throat

13. The amount of water eliminated daily through perspiration by the average person is   13._____
    approximately

    A. 2 to 3 quarts   B. 4 to 5 quarts
    C. 1/2 to 1 quart   D. none of the above

14. Another name for the disease rubella is   14._____

    A. chickenpox   B. German measles
    C. measles   D. vertigo

15. Of the following, the one associated with rheumatic fever is   15._____

    A. rheumatic palsy   B. coronary thrombosis
    C. St. Vitus dance   D. arteriosclerosis

16. The disease for which there is no vaccine for immunization at present is   16._____

    A. measles   B. smallpox
    C. poliomyelitis   D. infectious hepatitis

17. A communicable disease is apt to be MOST catching   17._____

    A. after the patient has seemingly recovered
    B. when it is being treated
    C. in its early stage
    D. when no prescribed medicine is taken by the afflicted person

18. In administering first aid care to a youngster suffering from convulsion, the CORRECT   18._____
    procedure to follow is to

    A. provide mild exercise such as walking
    B. apply hot wet-packs to the forehead
    C. provide a light body covering
    D. have the victim rest with feel elevated

19. Floor or scuff "burns" are examples of _____ wounds.   19._____

    A. abrasion   B. puncture
    C. laceration   D. incision

20. When applying an arm sling in cases of injury to the hand or lower forearm, the sling should be adjusted so that the hand is   20.____

    A. completely covered
    B. four inches above the level of the elbow
    C. on the same level as the elbow
    D. six inches below the level of the elbow

21. The first aid procedure recommended by the American Red Cross in the case of a poisonous sting on the finger is to   21.____

    A. use the cut and suction technique
    B. keep the hand in an elevated position
    C. apply a constricting band at the base of the finger
    D. apply heat to the area

22. Modern practice advises strongly against use of emetics in cases of poisoning by   22.____

    A. sleep inducing drugs   B. acids and alkalies
    C. strychnine   D. foods

23. The INITIAL action taken by a first aider in treating a case of severe bleeding is to   23.____

    A. apply pressure to the point nearest the injured part
    B. apply direct pressure on the wound
    C. apply a tourniquet
    D. elevate the injured part

24. The subclavian pressure point is used to control bleeding from the   24.____

    A. shoulder   B. lungs   C. chest   D. lower leg

25. The first aid procedure for strains is to   25.____

    A. massage the affected part vigorously
    B. apply warm, moist applications
    C. immediately immobilize the affected part
    D. bandage tightly to restrict movement

45

KEY (CORRECT ANSWERS)

1.	A		11.	D
2.	A		12.	B
3.	B		13.	A
4.	A		14.	B
5.	B		15.	C
6.	C		16.	D
7.	A		17.	C
8.	B		18.	C
9.	A		19.	A
10.	A		20.	B

21.	C
22.	B
23.	B
24.	A
25.	B

———

TEST 2

DIRECTIONS: Each question or incomplete statement is followed by several suggested answers or completions. Select the one that BEST answers the question or completes the statement. *PRINT THE LETTER OF THE CORRECT ANSWER IN THE SPACE AT THE RIGHT.*

1. The degree of shock resulting from a severe burn is dependent *primarily* upon the   1.____

    A. age of the person
    B. agent causing the burn
    C. body's resistance to burn
    D. extent of the area involved

2. In treating an electric shock victim, the FIRST thing the first aider should do is to   2.____

    A. send for a doctor
    B. determine whether the victim is still alive
    C. administer artificial respiration
    D. remove the victim from the current inducing mechanism

3. When taking the wrist pulse rate, one should   3.____

    A. have the patient hold his hand in a rigid position
    B. take the pulse with the thumb
    C. count the pulse-beats for 1 minute then check the rate by counting for another minute
    D. take the pulse on the "little finger side" of the wrist at the wrist bone

4. In all fracture cases, the IMMEDIATE objective of the first aider is to   4.____

    A. try to set the bone
    B. move the victim to a more comfortable position
    C. prevent further damage
    D. take the victim to a doctor or hospital

5. A fracture in which one side of a bone is broken while the other side is bent is known as a _____ fracture.   5.____

    A. Colles'   B. compound   C. comminuted   D. greenstick

6. The heart valve which prevents blood from flowing back into the right auricle is the   6.____

    A. tricuspid   B. aortic semilunar
    C. bicuspid   D. pulmonary semilunar

7. Blood pressure is associated with all of the following EXCEPT the   7.____

    A. viscosity of the blood
    B. force of the heart beat
    C. elasticity of the walls of the blood vessels
    D. number of leucocytes present in the blood

8. The clotting of blood is aided by   8.____

    A. calcium   B. phosphorus   C. copper   D. iron

9. A low red-blood cell count is generally an indication of   9.____

    A. leukemia   B. dermatitis
    C. anemia   D. myocarditis

10. The organ often referred to as the "graveyard of the red blood cells" is the   10.____

    A. spleen   B. bone marrow
    C. liver   D. heart

11. The body organ controlling the water content and osmotic pressure of the blood is the   11.____

    A. pancreas   B. kidneys
    C. lungs   D. stomach

12. Insulin is produced by the   12.____

    A. pituitary gland   B. pancreas
    C. parathyroid glands   D. adrenal glands

13. The _____ gland is known to regulate body metabolism.   13.____

    A. thymus   B. pineal
    C. thyroid   D. parotid

14. The MOST important secretion underlying the female sex drive is   14.____

    A. testosterone   B. estrin
    C. epinephrine   D. thyroxine

15. When fluid accumulates between the epidermis and dermis following irritation of a local   15.____
area, a _____ has formed.

    A. callous   B. boil   C. corn   D. blister

16. Nourishment for the hair comes entirely from the   16.____

    A. hair shaft   B. sebaceous glands
    C. blood   D. hair follicles

17. The hair and nails are outgrowths of   17.____

    A. dead tissue   B. the corium
    C. the epidermis   D. the subcutaneous tissue

18. Body balance is maintained by the   18.____

    A. ear drum   B. eustachian tube
    C. inner ear   D. semi-circular canals

19. The "power of accomodation" refers to the eyes' ability to   19.____

    A. discern colors
    B. adjust for peripheral vision
    C. discern shapes
    D. adjust for near or far vision

20. The portion of the eye containing nerve cells sensitive to light is the   20.____

    A. cornea   B. retina
    C. sclera   D. ciliary body

21. Astigmatism is due primarily to a(n)   21.____

    A. irregularity in the curvature of the eyeball
    B. loss of elasticity in the lens
    C. imbalance of eye muscles
    D. imperfect density of the acqueous humor

22. The term used to designate muscular imbalance of the eye is   22.____

    A. hyperopia   B. scleritis
    C. myopia   D. strabismus

23. The central portion of the tooth which contains blood vessels and nerves is called the   23.____

    A. cementum   B. pulp
    C. dentine   D. periodontal membrane

24. Malocclusion refers to   24.____

    A. teeth containing thin enamel
    B. deciduous teeth
    C. mottled teeth
    D. a crooked bite

25. In a full set of permanent teeth, the second molars lie between the   25.____

    A. second bicuspids and the cuspids
    B. wisdom teeth and the sixth-year molars
    C. first molars and the central incisors
    D. lateral incisors and the first bicuspids

KEY (CORRECT ANSWERS)

1.	D		11.	B
2.	D		12.	B
3.	C		13.	C
4.	C		14.	B
5.	D		15.	D
6.	A		16.	C
7.	D		17.	C
8.	A		18.	D
9.	C		19.	D
10.	A		20.	B

21.	A
22.	D
23.	B
24.	D
25.	B

TEST 3

DIRECTIONS: Each question or incomplete statement is followed by several suggested answers or completions. Select the one that BEST answers the question or completes the statement. *PRINT THE LETTER OF THE CORRECT ANSWER IN THE SPACE AT THE RIGHT.*

1.   A pupil receiving orthodontia care is having his   1._____

    A.   teeth cleaned   B.   gums treated
    C.   cavities filled   D.   teeth straightened

2.   It is MOST important to see that reducing diets of adolescents do NOT lack   2._____

    A.   simple sugars   B.   carbohydrates
    C.   fats   D.   proteins

3.   Of the following, the one considered the MAJOR cause of obesity is   3._____

    A.   too little exercise   B.   emotional disturbance
    C.   excessive eating   D.   inheritance

4.   The mineral that is essential to the process of oxidation by helping to carry oxygen to   4._____
every cell is

    A.   iodine   B.   sodium   C.   magnesium   D.   iron

5.   In the body, the interchange of food, oxygen and waste takes place in the   5._____

    A.   capillaries   B.   plasma
    C.   red blood cells   D.   lymph

6.   In nutrition, the utilization of absorbed products is called   6._____

    A.   osmosis   B.   metabolism
    C.   anabolism   D.   catabolism

7.   Of the following, the food HIGHEST in calorie value per pound is   7._____

    A.   lamb   B.   chocolate   C.   butter   D.   sugar

8.   Of the following foods, the one contributing MOST to growth and repair of tissue is   8._____

    A.   bread   B.   honey
    C.   string beans   D.   cheese

9.   The CHIEF value of cellulose in the diet is that it   9._____

    A.   provides an essential amino acid
    B.   is easily digested
    C.   gives bulk to the intestinal residues
    D.   is more soluble than starch

10.   In the human body, protein is stored in   10._____

    A.   the muscles   B.   body fat
    C.   the bone marrow   D.   no special part

11. Vitamin A deficiency is associated with all of the following EXCEPT   11.____

    A. retardation in the development of bones
    B. impairment of epithelial tissue
    C. faulty development of the teeth
    D. impairment of vision in dim light

12. Of the following, the BEST source of natural vitamin D is   12.____

    A. tomatoes   B. salmon
    C. eggs   D. green vegetables

13. The CORRECT association is   13.____

    A. rickets - niacin
    B. night blindness - ascorbic acid
    C. pellagra - vitamin D
    D. beriberi - thiamine

14. A serious disease chronic alcoholics are MOST subject to is   14.____

    A. diabetes   B. sinusitis
    C. bromidrosis   D. cirrhosis

15. One of the PRINCIPAL effects of nicotine upon the body is a(n)   15.____

    A. marked rise in blood pressure
    B. increase in the blood's capacity to carry oxygen
    C. marked increase in skin temperature
    D. increase in appetite

16. Of the following group of drugs, those *usually* referred to as "pep pills" are the   16.____

    A. amphetamines   B. hallucinogens
    C. opiates   D. barbiturates

17. All of the following are withdrawal symptoms a drug addict may experience EXCEPT   17.____

    A. muscle twitching
    B. cold skin covered with "gooseflesh"
    C. a decrease in the normal secretions of the body
    D. gnawing pains in the stomach accompanied by nausea and vomiting

18. In drug abuse, the *most commonly* used stimulant is   18.____

    A. seconal   B. benzedrine
    C. librium   D. nembutol

19. The opium derivative upon which the medical profession relies MOST to bring relief from pain is   19.____

    A. cocaine   B. heroin
    C. morphine   D. codeine

20. Of the following drugs, the ones which are synthetic substitutes for morphine are   20.____

    A. methadone and paregoric   B. methadone and dexamyl
    C. demerol and methadone   D. demerol and paregoric

21. Giving false reasons for one's behavior in order to preserve self-esteem is called   21.____

    A. sublimation   B. rationalization
    C. compensation   D. substitution

22. The most commonly used method for purifying large quantities of water is   22.____

    A. distillation   B. boiling
    C. ultraviolet irradiation   D. filtration

23. The author whose book SILENT SPRING caused wholesale governmental investigations   23.____
into chemical pesticides and pollution was

    A. Upton Sinclair   B. Albert Sabin
    C. Rachel Carson   D. Ralph Nader

24. Studies in Paris and Los Angeles showed that three-fourths of the air pollution came   24.____
from

    A. burning of trash, rubbish
    B. exhausts of jet airplanes
    C. incompletely burned gases of automobile exhausts
    D. factory waste

25. Ecology is a branch of science concerned with the   25.____

    A. reproduction aspects of body cells
    B. hereditary characteristics of chromosomes
    C. discovery and isolation of microscopic organisms
    D. interrelationship of organisms and their environments

KEY (CORRECT ANSWERS)

1.	D		11.	A
2.	D		12.	B
3.	C		13.	D
4.	D		14.	D
5.	A		15.	A
6.	C		16.	A
7.	C		17.	C
8.	D		18.	B
9.	C		19.	C
10.	D		20.	C

21.	B
22.	D
23.	C
24.	C
25.	D

EXAMINATION SECTION
TEST 1

DIRECTIONS: Each question or incomplete statement is followed by several suggested answers or completions. Select the one that BEST answers the question or completes the statement. *PRINT THE LETTER OF THE CORRECT ANSWER IN THE SPACE AT THE RIGHT.*

1. A specialist is a physician who has restricted his or her practice to a given body system. Which of the statements below is FALSE concerning the various medical specialties? A(n)   1._____

    A. internist deals with diseases of the bones
    B. opthamologist deals with diseases of the eye
    C. dermatologist deals with diseases of the skin
    D. neurologist deals with diseases of the brain and nervous system

2. Alcohol has which of the following effects on the body? Alcohol   2._____

    A. causes blood vessels near the skin to constrict
    B. helps the body retain heat
    C. stimulates responses by the brain
    D. stimulates the secretion of acid in the stomach

3. The term hypertension refers to someone who   3._____

    A. has high blood pressure
    B. has overtaxed his muscular system
    C. has stomach ulcers
    D. does not deal effectively with stress

4. When a person exhibits neurotic behavior, he may   4._____

    A. act in a peculiar way or exhibit physical symptoms because of his response to anxiety
    B. hallucinate and perceive objects around him to be different than they really are
    C. perceive reality in such a distorted way that he may be unable to function properly
    D. exhibit two widely different personalities or extremely different moods

5. Gonorrhea, the MOST frequently reported venereal disease,   5._____

    A. has early symptoms that are usually more pronounced in women than in men
    B. may be diagnosed by a blood test and treated with injections of gamma globulin
    C. is normally transmitted through sexual intercourse
    D. is caused and transferred by a virus

6. Which organ of the body is responsible for the oxidation of alcohol into simpler products? The   6._____

    A. heart   B. liver   C. lungs   D. stomach

7. Ovulation USUALLY occurs in the human female   7.____

    A. approximately five days before the end of the menstrual cycle
    B. approximately halfway between menstrual cycles
    C. during menstruation
    D. approximately five days after the beginning of menstruation

8. Which one of the following behaviors on the part of parents could be damaging to developing positive emotional health in children?   8.____

    A. Showing their love, support, and acceptance to their children
    B. Listening carefully to what their children have to say
    C. Setting no limits on what type of behaviors and actions are acceptable for their children
    D. Teaching the child to share with others and to consider others

9. When treating a person for shock, you should   9.____

    A. give the individual a stimulant to increase the blood pressure
    B. make sure the individual is sitting up to prevent fainting
    C. keep the individual warm and lying still
    D. place a pillow or other soft object under the individual's head to elevate this portion of the body

10. Most people will FIRST feel some effects from drinking alcoholic beverages when the percentage of alcohol in the blood reaches   10.____

    A. .02 to .05%   B. .5 to .7%
    C. 1 to 2%   D. .2 to .4%

11. Which drug below probably has the GREATEST tendency to be addictive?   11.____

    A. Heroin   B. Benzedrine
    C. Phenobarbital   D. Alcohol

12. It is important to apply a splint to a fractured limb before transporting a person because the splint will   12.____

    A. relieve the pain by keeping the limb immobile
    B. prevent the bones from growing together crookedly
    C. allow for limited use of the limb
    D. keep the bones immobile and prevent injury to muscles, blood vessels, and nerves

13. A person will never feel the intoxicating effects of alcohol if   13.____

    A. the rate at which alcohol is absorbed into the blood is greater than the rate at which the body oxidizes the alcohol
    B. the consumption of alcohol takes place slowly, but steadily
    C. the rate at which alcohol is absorbed into the blood is equal to the rate at which the body oxidizes the alcohol
    D. only beverages low in alcoholic content are consumed

14. Which of the following statements about the prevention and control of venereal disease is INCORRECT?   14.____

    A. If a person thinks he or she has been exposed to venereal disease, it is important to wait to see what symptoms develop before seeing a doctor.
    B. The probability of contracting venereal disease is greater when a person has many sexual partners.
    C. It is possible for venereal disease to be transmitted by kissing or by contact with open sores or broken skin.
    D. When a case of venereal disease is confirmed, it is important to discover the names of that person's sexual partner or partners.

15. The table below contains the basic information for Mr. Jones' diet on a daily basis. In addition, it is known that a reduction of 3,500 calories is required to lose one pound of fat. Using all this data, how many pounds would Mr. Jones lose in seven days?   15.____

Mr. Jones' basal metabolism	1600 cal/day
On his diet, Mr. Jones eats foods with a calorie content	1200 cal/day
Also on his diet, Mr. Jones has an exercise program in which he *burns up*	600 cal/day

_____ pound (s).

    A. Almost six   B. Two   C. One   D. Four

16. Which of the following is part of the male reproductive system?   16.____

    A. Fallopian tube   B. Vas deferens
    C. Cervix   D. Pineal gland

17. Under certain conditions, isometric exercise may be used as part of a fitness program to help develop   17.____

    A. strength   B. speed   C. endurance   D. flexibility

18. When considering the purchase of a health insurance policy, one should   18.____

    A. choose a policy that covers all routine costs
    B. avoid a policy that has a deductible clause
    C. choose a policy with the lowest premium cost
    D. choose a policy that covers the cost of medical services you can't afford

19. To aid yourself in developing positive emotional health, you should do all of the following EXCEPT   19.____

    A. attempt to resolve all problems by yourself and not not ask others for help
    B. use your own experiences as learning devices and modify your behavior accordingly
    C. develop a willingness to accept responsibility
    D. attempt to keep your body physically healthy

20. The PRIMARY purpose of Medicare is to help

    A. pay medical costs for the aged
    B. provide financial assistance to community health organizations
    C. pay medical costs of dependent children
    D. pay medical costs for the poor

20.____

21. A person who regularly takes narcotics commonly experiences all of the following EXCEPT

    A. reduced sexual drive or impotence
    B. constricted pupils
    C. diarrhea
    D. malnutrition

21.____

22. In the case of a severe burn that results in the blistering and charring of the skin, you should

    A. wash the area with soap and water to remove burned skin and prevent infection
    B. cover the burned area with a dry sterile dressing to reduce loss of body fluids
    C. remove fluid from blisters and cover with a clean sterile dressing
    D. cover the burned area with an ointment to reduce pain

22.____

23. Which drug or drug type in the list below can BEST be classified as a stimulant?

    A. Barbiturates   B. Amphetamines
    C. Alcohol   D. Opiates

23.____

24. The BEST emergency procedure to stop most cases of severe bleeding is to apply

    A. pressure directly over the wound
    B. a clean sterile bandage to the wound
    C. pressure at the closest pressure point
    D. a tourniquet

24.____

25. Some terms involving infectious disease are:
    I. Infection
    II. Invasion
    III. Incubation
What is the CORRECT order or sequence of these terms in regard to how an infectious disease affects the human body?

    A. II, I, III   B. I, II, III
    C. II, III, I   D. I, III, II

25.____

26. One of the procedures of CPR (cardio-pulmonary resuscitation) is external heart massage.
Which of the following statements about external heart massage is FALSE?
External heart massage

    A. is usually accompanied by mouth-to-mouth resuscitation
    B. squeezes the heart between the sternum and spine
    C. should only be given when there is no apparent carotid pulse
    D. should be given on a soft, unresistant surface to prevent injury to ribs

26.____

27. Which of the following is an effect of regular smoking?   27.____
Smoking

    A. increases the number of stillbirths in pregnant women
    B. tends to make it more difficult for the blood to clot
    C. reduces the chances of developing a stomach ulcer
    D. increases the appetite and stimulates the sense of smell

28. The emergency treatment to be used on a child who has swallowed a strong corrosive   28.____
substance should include all of the following EXCEPT

    A. treating the child for shock
    B. inducing vomiting
    C. calling a doctor or local hospital
    D. giving the child water or milk to drink

29. Carbon monoxide, one of the substances found in cigarette smoke, is thought to cause   29.____
shortness of breath because

    A. it is a depressant on the respiratory system
    B. it leaves a deposit of tar in the lungs
    C. it reduces the oxygen-carrying capacity of the blood
    D. hot carbon monoxide tends to singe the lung surfaces

30. The BEST way to choose a family doctor is to   30.____

    A. look for a physician closest to home
    B. consult the phone directory for a list of available physicians
    C. ask your local hospital or medical society for recommendations
    D. look in the advertisement section of the newspaper

KEY (CORRECT ANSWERS)

1.	A		16.	B
2.	D		17.	A
3.	A		18.	D
4.	A		19.	A
5.	C		20.	A
6.	B		21.	B
7.	B		22.	B
8.	C		23.	B
9.	C		24.	C
10.	A		25.	C
11.	A		26.	D
12.	D		27.	A
13.	C		28.	B
14.	C		29.	C
15.	B		30.	C

TEST 2

DIRECTIONS: Each question or incomplete statement is followed by several suggested answers or completions. Select the one that BEST answers the question or completes the statement. *PRINT THE LETTER OF THE CORRECT ANSWER IN THE SPACE AT THE RIGHT.*

1. Which of the following physiological changes commonly occurs in women during pregnancy?
The

    A. size of the heart is slightly reduced
    B. breasts increase in size
    C. position of the diaphragm is lowered
    D. breathing rate is lowered

1.____

2. The MAIN difference between aerobic and anaerobic exercise is that

    A. aerobic exercise is less suited to older persons than is anaerobic exercise
    B. aerobic exercise involves rapid and vigorous movements, while anaerobic exercise involves rhythmic and more fluid movements
    C. in aerobic exercise sufficient oxygen is present, but in anaerobic exercise, there is an oxygen deficiency
    D. aerobic exercise should be done no more than once a week to be most effective, while anaerobic exercise should be done more often

2.____

3. Cancer can BEST be defined as a(n)

    A. abnormal growth and spread of cells
    B. elevated white blood cell count
    C. viral infection
    D. fungus infection

3.____

4. To understand emotional responses, you should realize that

    A. your emotions cannot result in sickness
    B. your emotional responses are like reflexes that involve no thinking
    C. your emotional responses are related to your personal values
    D. you were born with the emotions you have now

4.____

5. Conception, or fertilization, in the human female

    A. requires implantation of the egg on the wall of the vagina
    B. requires one sperm to penetrate one egg
    C. takes place in the uterus
    D. takes place during menstruation

5.____

6. The MAJOR importance of fiber in the diet is that it

    A. provides energy for the body
    B. is a source of important minerals
    C. is extremely easy to digest
    D. helps in normal elimination

6.____

7. The incompatibility of the Rh blood factors in a pregnancy can be a problem when   7.____

    A. the mother is Rh positive and the father is Rh negative
    B. both the mother and father are Rh negative
    C. the mother is Rh negative and the baby is Rh positive
    D. both mother and baby are Rh negative

8. Which statement about vitamins is TRUE?   8.____

    A. The more vitamins you take, the more healthy your body will be.
    B. Some vitamins may be manufactured by the body.
    C. Vitamins are important sources of energy.
    D. Vitamins are a substitute for fats, proteins, and carbohydrates.

9. Below are listed some characteristics and symptoms of a common infectious disease: 9.____
    I. In the United States, its greatest incidence is among young people fifteen to nineteen years old.
    II. Symptoms may include fever, sore throat, nausea, and chills.
    III. A general weakness for three weeks to several months is common after the initial symptoms have passed.
    IV. A blood test can be used to diagnose the disease. From this information, you can diagnose this infectious disease as

    A. measles   B. mononucleosis
    C. hepatitis   D. pneumonia

10. Foods that are good sources of protein include   10.____

    A. fish, eggs, and cheese
    B. butter, margarine, and corn oil
    C. fruits and vegetables
    D. bread and cereal

11. An unborn human fetus receives nourishment through the   11.____

    A. amniotic fluid
    B. digestive system of the fetus
    C. lining of the uterus
    D. placenta

12. The MAJOR reason vegetarians must select a variety of foods is that   12.____

    A. vegetables are low in carbohydrates
    B. a wide variety of different enzymes is necessary in the digestive system
    C. eight essential amino acids are needed to build protein
    D. excesses of certain vitamins must be avoided

13. Which one of the following CANNOT be an infectious agent?   13.____

    A. Worms   B. Protozoa   C. Platelets   D. Fungus

14. The high consumption of foods that contain large amounts of saturated fats may represent a health hazard because these fats   14._____

    A. seem to increase the probability of developing cancer
    B. cause a build-up of fat-soluble vitamins in the body
    C. are thought to be a factor in heart disease
    D. accumulate in the liver and interfere with the production of bile

15. Which one of the following is considered to be a non-infectious disease?   15._____

    A. Pneumonia   B. Arthritis
    C. The common cold   D. Influenza

16. Defense mechanisms such as rationalization, repression, and escape   16._____

    A. represent responses that help reduce the stress of emotional conflict
    B. are signs of psychosis
    C. are effectively used when the emotional conflicts become overwhelming
    D. represent responses that help reduce the stress of emotional conflict

17. The endocrine glands serve an important function in the body by   17._____

    A. producing substances that carry nerve impulses
    B. producing hormones which regulate many body processes
    C. helping to regulate a person's genetic make-up
    D. releasing disease-fighting agents directly into the bloodstream

18. Which of the statements below is TRUE concerning cancer?   18._____

    A. A *pap smear* is an effective treatment for cancer.
    B. A lump in a woman's breast means she has cancer.
    C. Early diagnosis is important to cure cancer.
    D. Most skin cancers are fatal.

19. In any well-constructed weight-reducing diet, a person should   19._____

    A. only eat foods that contain no calories
    B. eliminate all favorite foods to reduce calorie intake
    C. strive for a weight loss of no more than one or two pounds per week
    D. reduce the amount of strenuous physical activity

20. Since syphilis is a serious venereal disease among young people, it is IMPORTANT to know that   20._____

    A. if left untreated even after many years, syphilis causes only minor physical damage
    B. syphilis is difficult to treat, even with antibiotics
    C. once a person is cured of syphilis, the body's immune system prevents that person from becoming reinfected
    D. the first symptom of the disease is often a sore or lesion in the genital region

21. The health hazards of being overweight include   21._____

    A. increased chances of becoming anemic
    B. severely reduced blood pressure
    C. increased chances of developing heart disease
    D. the likelihood of vitamin deficiencies

22. One of the changes that occurs in both boys and girls during puberty is   22.____

    A. improved physical coordination
    B. decreased hormone production
    C. increased amount of body hair
    D. reduced rate of growth

23. Which one of the following statements listed concerning a person's emotional health is   23.____
TRUE?

    A. Emotionally healthy people do not experience anxiety.
    B. Emotionally healthy people have no psychological needs.
    C. Emotional health is measured by a set of exact standards.
    D. Emotionally healthy people may avoid situations that will cause them to become anxious.

24. Antibodies, which help fight disease in the body, are   24.____

    A. proteins manufactured by the body's white cells that react against disease organisms or their toxins
    B. drugs, produced in other living things, which, when injected into the body, help kill disease organisms or their toxins
    C. living infectious agents that are used in vaccines to stimulate the body's immune response
    D. substances from outside the body that stimulate the body's immune response

25. The material found in cigarette smoke that contains the MOST carcinogens is   25.____

    A. tar   B. ammonia   C. ash   D. nicotine

26. The MAIN function of the digestive organ indicated by the arrow in the diagram below is   26.____

    A. absorption of essential nutrients
    B. absorption of water
    C. secretion of digestive enzymes
    D. secretion of hydrochloric acid

27. To reduce the likelihood of developing cardiovascular disease, one should   27.____

    A. keep busy working and only rarely relax
    B. eliminate exercise to avoid straining the heart
    C. eliminate or reduce cigarette smoking
    D. eat plenty of butter, milk, eggs, and cheese

28. When people smoke, the nicotine in tobacco tends to cause a(n)   28._____

    A. sharp decrease in a person's blood pressure
    B. constricting of the blood vessels
    C. decrease in the heartbeat
    D. increase in temperature in the fingers and toes

29. When purchasing a prescription drug, why should you ask the pharmacist whether the   29._____
drug has a generic equivalent?
Generic equivalent drugs

    A. are more pure than the brand-name drug
    B. usually have fewer bad side effects than the brand-name drug
    C. are designed to give you a higher dosage
    D. are usually less expensive than brand-name drugs

30. In any weight-reducing diet, the nutritional calorie is of interest to the dieter.   30._____
The nutritional calorie is

    A. found in larger amounts in protein than in any other basic nutrient
    B. a measure of the amount of body fat
    C. found in everything we eat or drink
    D. considered as a unit that measures the amount of fuel entering the body

---

KEY (CORRECT ANSWERS)

1.	B		16.	A
2.	B		17.	B
3.	A		18.	C
4.	C		19.	C
5.	B		20.	D
6.	D		21.	C
7.	C		22.	C
8.	B		23.	D
9.	B		24.	A
10.	A		25.	A
11.	D		26.	B
12.	A		27.	C
13.	C		28.	B
14.	C		29.	D
15.	B		30.	D

EXAMINATION SECTION
TEST 1

DIRECTIONS: Each question or incomplete statement is followed by several suggested answers or completions. Select the one that BEST answers the question or completes the statement. *PRINT THE LETTER OF THE CORRECT ANSWER IN THE SPACE AT THE RIGHT.*

1. Which one of the following is classified as a fissure of the brain?   1._____

    A. Maxillary plexuses   B. Periphlebitis
    C. Visceral cleavage   D. Parieto-occipital sulcus

2. Paralysis of corresponding parts on two sides of the body is known as   2._____

    A. diplegia   B. hemiplegia   C. monoplegia   D. hemiparesis

3. Muscular dystrophy is a condition in which   3._____

    A. the cause is known
    B. there is apparently no hereditary transmission
    C. several members of the family are often affected in the same manner
    D. the juvenile type is rarely found in boys

4. Tachycardia is a condition of the _____ system.   4._____

    A. skeletal   B. endocrine
    C. circulatory   D. digestive

5. Which one of the following diseases involves the lymph nodes and has a poor prognosis?   5._____

    A. Colitis   B. Ileitis
    C. Lordosis   D. Hodgkin's disease

6. Of the following diseases, the one that is NOT directly attributable to a specific vitamin deficiency is   6._____

    A. scurvy   B. beriberi   C. tularemia   D. pellagra

7. The three bones known as the *hammer, anvil,* and *stirrup* are found in the human   7._____

    A. nose   B. knee   C. ear   D. elbow

8. Of the following body functions, the one performed by the white blood cells is   8._____

    A. carrying carbon dioxide to the lungs
    B. destroying invading bacteria
    C. carrying food particles to the cells
    D. destroying old red blood corpuscles

9. Of the following, the word *dyspnea* is MOST closely associated with   9._____

    A. bronchial asthma   B. meningitis
    C. rickets   D. synovitis

10. A disease characterized by tonic spasms in the voluntarily moved muscles is

   A. osteomyelitis
   B. otomycosis
   C. pleuralgia
   D. myotonia congenita

10.____

11. With which one of the following is the term *aura* MOST commonly associated?

   A. Psycho-motor seizures
   B. Petit mal seizures
   C. Grand mal seizures
   D. Laryngospasm

11.____

12. *A short lapse of consciousness and a sudden momentary pause in conversation or movement* is MOST suggestive of

   A. nephrosis
   B. autism
   C. Friedreich's ataxia
   D. petit mal seizure

12.____

13. Which one of the following diseases usually has a very poor prognosis?

   A. Hodgkin's disease
   B. Slipped epiphsys
   C. Cerebral palsy
   D. Eczema

13.____

14. Mononucleosis is an abnormal condition of the

   A. blood
   B. liver
   C. nerves
   D. colon

14.____

15. Increased thirst, increased urination, loss of weight, and general fatigue are common symptoms of

   A. arthrogryposis
   B. diabetes
   C. hepatitis
   D. arthritis

15.____

16. Dementia praecox is now commonly called _____ reaction.

   A. schizophrenic
   B. depressive
   C. manic
   D. obsessive

16.____

17. Which one of the following is a disease of the ear?

   A. Ostitis
   B. Otitis
   C. Omphalitis
   D. Ophthalmia

17.____

18. Glomerulonephritis is a disease of the

   A. heart
   B. stomach
   C. kidney
   D. larynx

18.____

19. Which one of the following is the disease that would MOST likely impair the ability to ambulate?

   A. Diabetes
   B. Colitis
   C. Bronchiectasis
   D. Spina bifida

19.____

20. The lay term *hunchback* is synonymous with

   A. kyphosis
   B. scoliosis
   C. torticollis
   D. spondylolisthesis

20.____

21. Which one of the following diseases involves a malformation of the heart?

   A. Hydrocele
   B. Tetralogy of Fallot
   C. Myasthenia gravis
   D. Lordosis

21.____

64

22. Of the following, the disease which would be included under the general classification *orthopedic* is   22.____

    A. lupus erythematosus   B. lymphedema
    C. Osgood-Schlatter's   D. opthalmospasm

23. Of the following cardiac classifications, the one the teacher would be LEAST likely to encounter is   23.____

    A. 4A   B. 3C   C. 4E   D. 2C

24. The name Cooley is MOST closely associated with a form of   24.____

    A. anemia   B. dystrophy
    C. asthma   D. cerebral palsy

25. Chorea is a disease of the _____ system.   25.____

    A. digestive   B. respiratory
    C. circulatory   D. nervous

26. Rickets results from a lack of calcium and of vitamin   26.____

    A. A   B. C   C. D   D. E

27. Recommended foods to alleviate rickets should include   27.____

    A. leafy vegetables, meat, fruits
    B. bread, cereals, dried beans
    C. tomatoes, apricots, green vegetables
    D. canned salmon, liver, whole milk

28. Which one of the following diseases is ALWAYS congenital?   28.____

    A. Cerebral palsy   B. Osteogenesis imperfecta
    C. Rheumatoid arthritis   D. Pericarditis

29. Of the following, which condition represents a disturbance of the neuro-muscular system frequently accompanied by perceptual difficulties?   29.____

    A. Perthe's disease   B. Cerebral palsy
    C. Spina bifida   D. Talipes

30. The following symptoms are noted in a group of children: enlargement of the calf muscles, difficulty in raising arms, afflicted shoulder and face muscles, waddling gait. The children are *probably* suffering from   30.____

    A. spina bifida   B. polio
    C. muscular dystrophy   D. Perthe's disease

31. Of the following diseases, which one is hereditary?   31.____

    A. Scoliosis   B. Osteomyelitis
    C. Hemophilia   D. Chorea

32. In which one of the following diseases is overweight frequently a concomitant?   32.____

    A. Pott's disease   B. Epilepsy
    C. Slipped epiphysis   D. Coxa vara

33. Hyperactivity is MOST apt to be observed in children who have   33.____

    A. muscular dystrophy   B. brain damage
    C. ileitis   D. rheumatic fever

34. Three broad categories of physical disabilities—orthopedic, cardiac, and chronic—are   34.____
often used for convenience in classifying children in health conservation classes.
The group below which BEST fits into the category of *chronic* is

    A. rheumatic fever, muscular dystrophy, kyphosis
    B. nephrosis, colitis, hepatitis
    C. Friedreich's ataxia, osteomyelitis, torticollis
    D. rickets, chorea, arthogryposis

35. The one of the following diseases which is the *leading* cause of death in the 10- to 15-   35.____
year age group is

    A. cancer   B. poliomyelitis
    C. diabetes   D. rheumatic fever

36. The one of the following which would MOST likely be a result of untreated syphilis is   36.____

    A. paresis   B. phlebitis   C. carcinoma   D. silicosis

37. The one of the following which is MOST likely to be used in establishing a diagnosis of   37.____
epilepsy is a(n)

    A. electrocardiogram   B. spinal x-ray
    C. fluoroscopic examination   D. electroencephalogram

38. The pathology of diabetes involves the failure of the body to produce an adequate supply   38.____
of

    A. sugar   B. carbohydrates   C. insulin   D. salt

39. The one of the following statements which is TRUE about diabetes is that   39.____

    A. it can generally be cured if medical orders are followed
    B. it can generally be kept under control but not cured
    C. it is an infectious disease
    D. blindness is an inevitable result of it

40. Scurvy is caused by a deficiency of vitamin   40.____

    A. A   B. B   C. C   D. K

41. The one of the following diseases which is covered by benefits under the Worker's   41.____
Compensation Law is

    A. syphilis   B. diabetes
    C. poliomyelitis   D. silicosis

42. The one of the following vitamins which is used as an aid in coagulating blood is vitamin   42.____

    A. A   B. B   C. C   D. K

43. The one of the following statements which is TRUE of progressive muscular dystrophy is   43._____
that

    A. it is transmitted to the male children through the mother
    B. the male is the carrier of the disease
    C. the brain is primarily affected because of a lack of blood supply
    D. it is caused by a nutritional deficiency in the ante-partum period

44. If a patient is repeatedly admitted to the hospital because of a series of mishaps in which   44._____
he has suffered broken bones, the one of the following which is MOST likely to be true is
that he is

    A. a rigid person   B. a diabetic
    C. malingering   D. accident-prone

45. The one of the following groups of illnesses which is known to be caused by bacteria is   45._____
_____ diseases.

    A. mental   B. acute infectious
    C. nutritional   D. degenerative

46. The one of the following with which Hodgkin's disease is commonly associated is   46._____

    A. neurasthenia   B. meningitis
    C. poliomyelitis   D. cancer

47. The one of the following diseases in which the determination of the sedimentation rate is   47._____
important for diagnostic purposes is

    A. rheumatic heart disease
    B. congenital heart disease
    C. hypertensive heart disease
    D. diabetes

48. The one of the following disease classifications which would include spinal meningitis is   48._____

    A. cancer or tumor
    B. nutritional disease
    C. acute infectious disease
    D. focal or local infection

49. The one of the following diseases which may cause visual impairment and blindness is   49._____

    A. ringworm   B. osteomyelitis
    C. poliomyelitis   D. diabetes

50. The one of the following which is NOT an anesthetic is   50._____

    A. cholesterol   B. nitrous oxide
    C. sodium pentothal   D. procaine

KEY (CORRECT ANSWERS)

1.	D	11.	C	21.	B	31.	C	41.	D
2.	A	12.	D	22.	C	32.	C	42.	D
3.	C	13.	A	23.	A	33.	B	43.	A
4.	C	14.	A	24.	A	34.	B	44.	D
5.	D	15.	B	25.	D	35.	D	45.	B
6.	C	16.	A	26.	C	36.	A	46.	D
7.	C	17.	B	27.	D	37.	D	47.	A
8.	B	18.	C	28.	B	38.	C	48.	C
9.	A	19.	D	29.	B	39.	B	49.	D
10.	D	20.	A	30.	C	40.	C	50.	A

———

TEST 2

DIRECTIONS: Each question or incomplete statement is followed by several suggested answers or completions. Select the one that BEST answers the question or completes the statement. *PRINT THE LETTER OF THE CORRECT ANSWER IN THE SPACE AT THE RIGHT.*

1. The one of the following which is MOST likely to be an occupational disease is   1._____

   A. cancer   B. cerebral hemorrhage
   C. septicemia   D. arsenic poisoning

2. The one of the following which is a nutritional disease is   2._____

   A. tuberculosis   B. rickets
   C. bubonic plague   D. typhoid fever

3. Tachycardia is a condition o the _____ system.   3._____

   A. skeletal   B. endocrine
   C. circulatory   D. digestive

4. Which one of the following diseases involves the lymph nodes and has a poor prognosis?   4._____

   A. Colitis   B. Ileitis
   C. Lordosis   D. Hodgkin's disease

5. Which of the following diseases has yielded to chemotherapeutic treatment in recent years?   5._____

   A. Multiple sclerosis   B. Tuberculosis
   C. Diabetes   D. Scleroderma

6. The MOST satisfactory results in the treatment of epilepsy have been obtained through the use of   6._____

   A. vitamins   B. diet   C. drugs   D. exercise

7. In former years, all members of the family of a child with a communicable disease were quarantined.
   At the present time, the child's siblings may attend school unless the disease in question is   7._____

   A. diphtheria   B. whooping cough
   C. mumps   D. ringworm

8. The CHIEF purpose of the Snellen test is   8._____

   A. diagnosis   B. screening
   C. placement   D. prognosis

9. During the daily health observation period, the teacher notices that a child has evidence of pediculosis.
   The teacher should   9._____

   A. isolate the child from the group
   B. send for a parent and explain the seriousness of the situation

    C.   give a talk on the subject to the class
    D.   refer the child to the principal for possible exclusion

10.   Which one of the following diseases may result in brain damage?   10._____

    A.   Poliomyelitis   B.   Lymphadenoma
    C.   Spondylitis   D.   Encephalitis

11.   A disease usually characterized by frequent vomiting and cramps is   11._____

    A.   colitis   B.   bronchitis
    C.   myocarditis   D.   empyemia

12.   A lateral curvature of the spine is characteristic of   12._____

    A.   scoliosis   B.   lordosis   C.   hyphosis   D.   stenosis

13.   Which of the following is one of the great dangers of many forms of anemia?   13._____

    A.   Brain deterioration   B.   Secondary infection
    C.   Mental deficiency   D.   Bleeding

14.   A cleft of the vertebral column with meningeal protrusion is characteristic of   14._____

    A.   Sprengel's deformity   B.   scoliosis
    C.   coxa vara   D.   spina bifida

15.   When correctly used, the term *allergen* refers to   15._____

    A.   a person who is allergic
    B.   an antihistamine medication
    C.   a substance which produces allergy
    D.   the tendency to inherit an allergy

16.   Which of the following is congenital?   16._____

    A.   Meningitis   B.   Gastroenteritis
    C.   Chronic bronchitis   D.   Osteogenesis imperfecta

17.   Spasm is a common characteristic of   17._____

    A.   slipped epiphysis   B.   otitis
    C.   muscular dystrophy   D.   asthma

18.   Which one of the following is MOST likely to be associated with production of large quan-   18._____
      tities of mucous?

    A.   Kyphosis   B.   Bronchiectasis
    C.   Lymphodenoma   D.   Thyroid deficiency

19.   Poor bladder control is MOST frequently associated with   19._____

    A.   rheumatic fever   B.   hemophilia
    C.   club foot   D.   torticollis

20.   Excessive accumulation of cerebrospinal fluid within the skull is usually characterized as   20._____

    A.   mongolism   B.   microcephaly
    C.   macrocephaly   D.   hydrocephaly

21. Cerebral palsy is a term applied to a group of conditions having in common   21.____

    A. hereditary malformation
    B. retarded mentality
    C. microcephalic appearance
    D. disorders of muscular control

22. Which one of the following conditions is caused by the inflammation of the lower part of   22.____
    the intestine?

    A. Pyelitis   B. Transverse myelitis
    C. Regional ileitis   D. Hepatitis

23. In contrast with former treatment methods that called for intramuscular injections, oral   23.____
    medication is now frequently provided for treating

    A. diabetes   B. colitis
    C. thyroiditis   D. myelitis

24. A child who has cerebral palsy has difficulty in keeping his paper on his desk.   24.____
    Which one of the following materials should his teacher provide to help him?

    A. A thick piece of oaktag   B. A paperweight
    C. Masking tape   D. A set of tacks

25. A bone fracture which is in the process of healing will call for greater intake of   25.____

    A. vitamin B complex   B. folic acid
    C. vitamins D and C   D. vitamins A and K

26. Antihistamines are often used in treating   26.____

    A. allergies   B. anemias
    C. glandular fevers   D. adrenal hemorrhages

27. A cardiac child classified as 4E would be MOST apt to   27.____

    A. be placed in a health conservation class
    B. receive home instruction
    C. be placed in a regular class with limited physical activity
    D. be placed in a regular class following a short stay in a special class

28. An underweight child with a cardiac condition should be encouraged to   28.____

    A. add candy to his diet
    B. add carbohydrates such as bread and milk desserts to his diet
    C. maintain weight below normal since this insures a margin of safety should illness
        occur
    D. increase his intake of fluids and salt

29. Which one of the following involves the degeneration of parts of the brain, or spinal   29.____
    chord, or both?

    A. Schizophrenia   B. Spina bifida
    C. Multiple sclerosis   D. Pott's disease

71

30. Of the following, the disability with the BEST prognosis is   30.____

   A. Cooley's anemia   B. encephalitis
   C. hemophilia   D. slipped epiphyses

31. Infectious mononucleosis is also known as   31.____

   A. Hodgkin's disease   B. glandular fever
   C. chorea   D. bronchiectasis

32. Which one of the following is non-inflammatory?   32.____

   A. Cystitis   B. Nephritis
   C. Nephrosis   D. Pyelitis

33. Idiopathic epilepsy may be BEST characterized as a condition which   33.____

   A. is of unknown origin
   B. is a result of some trauma
   C. is not amenable to treatment
   D. may be safely ignored

34. Which one of the following conditions is characterized by loss of weight, sleeplessness,   34.____
irritability, and bulging eyes?

   A. Tuberculosis   B. Overactive thyroid
   C. Myasthenia gravis   D. Frederick's ataxia

35. Cardiac involvement may result from a previous acute, infectious disease.   35.____
The disease referred to is

   A. streptococcus sore throat   B. measles
   C. uremia   D. enteric fever

36. A type of facial paralysis due to a neuritis of the facial nerve in the Fallopian canal is   36.____
called

   A. Paget's disease   B. Bell's palsy
   C. endocarditis   D. encephalitis

37. A slipped epiphysis occurs MOST frequently in   37.____

   A. early adolescence   B. late adolescence
   C. pre-adolescence   D. early childhood

38. An electroencephalogram would NOT ordinarily be used in connection with   38.____

   A. epilepsy   B. ataxia   C. pyelitis   D. meningitis

39. Which of the following is characterized by lifeless muscle?   39.____

   A. Pott's disease   B. Flaccid paralysis
   C. Scoliosis   D. Colitis

40. The psychologist's report on a child states that he suffers from aphasia.   40.____
Aphasia is a(n)

   A. impairment of the ability to use or understand spoken language
   B. disturbance of muscular coordination

C.   neurotic reaction characterized by intense fear
D.   inability consciously to recall events or personal identity

41.   Which one of the following BEST defines *a suffix of nouns denoting a morbid condition of growth*?   41._____

   A.   Oma   B.   Itis   C.   Osis   D.   Omy

42.   The formation of an artificial anus in the anterior abdominal wall or loin is known as a(n)   42._____

   A.   anuria   B.   achondroplasia
   C.   colostomy   D.   plastogene

43.   Carpus, ethmoid, and coccyx are   43._____

   A.   arteries   B.   bones   C.   enzymes   D.   ligaments

44.   Inflammation of the intestinal tract is known as   44._____

   A.   enteritis   B.   hepatitis
   C.   glomerulonephritis   D.   rhinitis

45.   For the past twenty years, the leading cause of death in children has been   45._____

   A.   rheumatic fever   B.   poliomyelitis
   C.   cancer   D.   heart disease

46.   Of the following, which one is the MOST frequent cause of long-term crippling conditions in children?   46._____

   A.   Infections   B.   Congenital defects
   C.   Metabolic disturbances   D.   Unknown causes

47.   Which one of the following statements concerning rheumatic fever and heart disease is CORRECT?   47._____

   A.   All children who have rheumatic fever will have heart disease.
   B.   Some children who have had rheumatic fever will have heart disease.
   C.   No children who have had rheumatic fever will have heart disease.
   D.   All children with heart disease have had rheumatic fever.

48.   Polyarthritis is sometimes used as a synonym for   48._____

   A.   acute rheumatic fever   B.   arthrochondritis
   C.   multiple sclerosis   D.   polyneuritis

49.   Pfeiffer's disease, glandular fever, and infectious mononucleosis are all   49._____

   A.   the same disease
   B.   non-communicable diseases
   C.   characterized by a decrease in abnormal mononuclear cells
   D.   the result of an intestinal virus

50.   Prolongation of the blood clotting time results from a deficiency of vitamin   50._____

   A. B_2 B.   K   C.   E   D.   D

73

KEY (CORRECT ANSWERS)

1.	D	11.	A	21.	D	31.	B	41.	A
2.	B	12.	A	22.	C	32.	C	42.	C
3.	C	13.	B	23.	A	33.	A	43.	B
4.	D	14.	D	24.	C	34.	B	44.	A
5.	B	15.	C	25.	C	35.	A	45.	D
6.	C	16.	C	26.	A	36.	B	46.	B
7.	A	17.	D	27.	B	37.	A	47.	B
8.	B	18.	C	28.	B	38.	C	48.	A
9.	D	19.	A	29.	C	39.	B	49.	A
10.	D	20.	D	30.	D	40.	A	50.	B

———

TEST 3

DIRECTIONS: Each question or incomplete statement is followed by several suggested answers or completions. Select the one that BEST answers the question or completes the statement. *PRINT THE LETTER OF THE CORRECT ANSWER IN THE SPACE AT THE RIGHT.*

1. Of the following, the one which is NOT a symptom of shock is a   1._____

   A. cool, clammy skin   B. weak pulse
   C. flushed face   D. feeling of weakness

2. It is INCORRECT to state that the procedure of exercise that causes fatigue is   2._____

   A. sarcolactic acid   B. acid potassium phosphate
   C. carbon dioxide   D. glycogen

3. Of the following diseases or eruptions, the one which is non-communicable is   3._____

   A. ringworm   B. chicken pox
   C. pink eye   D. eczema

4. The so-called *fuel* foods used by the body are largely made up of   4._____

   A. vitamins   B. fats
   C. proteins   D. carbohydrates

5. The type of wound resulting from a floor burn is known as a(n)   5._____

   A. laceration   B. abrasion   C. incision   D. puncture

6. Of the following foods, the one *generally* considered to be RICHEST in minerals is   6._____

   A. fruit   B. pastry   C. cereal   D. meat

7. The pressure point MOST effective in controlling arterial bleeding of the forearm is located   7._____

   A. near the wrist
   B. near the elbow
   C. on the outer surface of the upper arm halfway between the shoulder and the elbow
   D. behind the inner end of the collarbone

8. According to the American Red Cross, carbon monoxide causes death by   8._____

   A. combining more readily with the red blood cells than oxygen does and thus depriving the body of oxygen
   B. destroying the red blood cells
   C. searing the air sacs of the lungs and preventing oxygen from entering the blood
   D. paralyzing the muscles that function in respiration

9. In the event of an emergency need for an ambulance, we should FIRST call the   9._____

   A. police   B. hospital
   C. health department   D. fire department

10. A direct blow upon a muscle produces a   10._____

    A. sprain   B. fracture   C. contusion   D. strain

11. The Health Department reports that, of the following, the cause of the GREATEST number of deaths in New York was   11.____

    A. accidents
    B. heart disease
    C. cancer
    D. diabetes

12. Upon discovering two members of the center smoking cigarettes on a stairway, you should   12.____

    A. take them to an exit and make certain they leave the building
    B. tell them to put out the lighted cigarettes and, in the future, to step outside the building to smoke
    C. warn them that smoking is forbidden and they are liable to arrest
    D. None of the above

13. Congenital malformation of the brain is often associated with   13.____

    A. hydrocephaly
    B. myelitis
    C. varicella
    D. lupus erythematosus

14. The use of an electroencephalogram *usually* proves MOST valuable in the diagnosis of   14.____

    A. epilepsy
    B. osteoma
    C. lordosis
    D. nephritis

15. Incontinence is MOST often an accompanying symptom of   15.____

    A. spina bifida
    B. lordosis
    C. Friedreich's ataxia
    D. Hodgkin's disease

16. Of the following, the MOST frequently observed preliminary indication of illness among children is   16.____

    A. fever
    B. listlessness
    C. skin rash
    D. coughing

17. Inflammation of the intestinal tract is known as   17.____

    A. enteritis
    B. hepatitis
    C. glomerulonephritis
    D. rhinitis

18. Which one of the following conditions is CORRECTLY paired with an associated disability often found as a secondary defect?   18.____

    A. Cerebral palsy - hearing defect
    B. Chorea - visual defect
    C. Perthe's disease - speech defect
    D. Torticollis - poor coordination

19. In which one of the following pairs is it MOST difficult to arrive at a differential diagnosis?   19.____

    A. Encephalitis - meningitis
    B. Aphasia - brain damage
    C. Poliomyelitis - muscular dystrophy
    D. Hydrocephalia - microcephalia

20. Abnormal brain wave discharges are MOST characteristic of
    20.____

    A. diabetes   B. epilepsy   C. herpes   D. Hansen's dis-
                                                      ease

21. Polyarthritis is sometimes used as a synonym for
    21.____

    A. acute rheumatic fever   B. arthrochondritis
    C. multiple sclerosis   D. polyneuritis

22. Pfeiffer's disease, glandular fever, and infectious mononucleosis are all
    22.____

    A. the same disease
    B. non-communicable diseases
    C. characterized by a decrease in abnormal mononuclear cells
    D. the result of an intestinal virus

23. Prolongation of the blood clotting time results from a deficiency of vitamin
    23.____

    A. B_2 B. K   C. E   D. D

24. Rheumatic fever may affect the body in all of the following ways EXCEPT by
    24.____

    A. attacking the connective tissues of the body
    B. scarring the heart valves
    C. causing inflammation of the inner lining of the heart
    D. forming a clot of blood within the heart

25. A pupil who has been excluded from school because of scarlet fever may be readmitted
    25.____
    upon presentation of a note from the

    A. school nurse   B. department of health
    C. family physician   D. any of the above

26. In regard to polio immunity, all of the following statements are correct EXCEPT:
    26.____

    A. Both the gamma globulin and the Salk vaccine protect against three known types
       of polio virus
    B. Gamma globulin is a mixture of antibodies against polio, while the Salk vaccine is a
       vaccination in which mild forms of the viruses are given
    C. The Salk vaccine is designed to give longer acquired immunity than the gamma
       globulin
    D. Gamma globulin is obtained only from the blood of persons who have recovered
       from polio

27. All of the following terms are associated with cancer EXCEPT
    27.____

    A. scotoma   B. carcinoma   C. sarcoma   D. myeloma

28. Hemolytic streptococci are associated with all of the following EXCEPT
    28.____

    A. septic sore throat   B. rheumatic fever
    C. scarlet fever   D. tuberculosis

29. All of the following statements concerning viruses are correct EXCEPT:
    29.____

    A. Viruses are harder to kill than ordinary bacteria.

B. Viruses depend upon living cells for food.
C. Virus cultures can be set up with surviving cells.
D. Most of the antibiotics destroy viruses.

30. Of the following diseases, the one caused by protozoa is   30.____

    A. amebic dysentary   B. trichinosis
    C. hookworm   D. botulism

31. All of the following statements concerning epilepsy are correct EXCEPT: 31.____

    A. Seizures in about 50% of children with this condition can be controlled
    B. The correlation of epilepsy with mental retardation is relatively high
    C. The incidence of epilepsy is higher than that of polio
    D. Encephalographs have proved helpful in the diagnosis of epileptic seizures

32. All of the following associations are correct EXCEPT: 32.____

    A. William Menninger - heart surgery
    B. Elie Metchnikoff - function of white blood cells in engulfing and destroying bacteria
    C. Joseph Lister - use of antiseptics in surgery
    D. Alexander Fleming - effect of pencillium on growth bacteria

33. A person suffering from heterophoria may find that because of his condition,   33.____

    A. he is not able to walk rapidly without distress
    B. his reflexes have become slower
    C. his eyes have a tendency to turn away from the position of binocular vision
    D. he has difficulty in hearing high pitch sounds

34. Bell's palsy usually affects the   34.____

    A. abdominal area   B. chest
    C. lower extremities   D. facial area

35. All of the following associations are correct EXCEPT: 35.____

    A. Histology - science which deals with tissues
    B. Pathology - science which deals with the nature of disease
    C. Cytology - science which deals with cells
    D. Geomedicine - science which deals with old age and its diseases

36. All of the following are symptoms of disorders of the circulatory system EXCEPT   36.____

    A. dyspnea   B. hypertension   C. enteritis   D. cyanosis

37. The grouping of types of human blood is based upon the   37.____

    A. platelets   B. red corpuscles
    C. white corpuscles   D. thrombocytes

38. A vaccine is introduced into the body PRIMARILY to   38.____

    A. kill the causative organism
    B. stimulate the growth of specific antibodies
    C. inhibit the growth of the causative organism
    D. produce bacteriostasis

39. All of the following are recommended by the National Foot Health Council for children's shoes EXCEPT: 39.____

   A. Since the normal foot is springy and acts as a shock absorber, rubber-soled shoes are preferred to leather-soled shoes
   B. A counter of leather around the heel is preferable to any other material
   C. Shoes should be narrow at the top of the heel, yet wide enough at the base to provide pivoting room for the broad base of the heel bone
   D. A cloth lining over the toes should be provided to absorb moisture

40. All of the following advances in medicine occurred during the last fifty years EXCEPT the   40.____

   A. discovery that malignant cells can live without oxygen
   B. regulation by vitamin C of the rate at which cholesterol is formed
   C. use of typhoid fever vaccine for cases of encephalitis
   D. conversion of normal cells into cancer cells in test tubes

41. The one of the following which is MOST frequently the cause of cerebral palsy is   41.____

   A. an infectious disease   B. a birth injury
   C. a hereditary defect   D. poor nutrition

42. The one of the following conditions which is due to dysfunction of the thyroid gland is   42.____

   A. cholecystitis   B. cretinism
   C. congenital syphilis   D. epilepsy

43. Enuresis is MOST frequently a symptom of   43.____

   A. kidney infection   B. emotional problems
   C. poor personal hygiene   D. carelessness

44. The one of the following which is MOST frequently used in establishing a diagnosis of epilepsy is a(n)   44.____

   A. electroencephalogram   B. complete blood count
   C. electrocardiogram   D. glucose tolerance test

45. The one of the following which is NOT infectious is   45.____

   A. pulmonary tuberculosis   B. poliomyelitis
   C. syphilis   D. muscular dystrophy

46. For the past twenty years, the leading cause of death in children has been   46.____

   A. rheumatic fever   B. poliomyelitis
   C. cancer   D. heart disease

47. Of the following, which one is the MOST frequent cause of long-term crippling conditions in children?   47.____

   A. Infections   B. Congenital defects
   C. Metabolic disturbances   D. Unknown causes

48. Which one of the following statements concerning rheumatic fever and heart disease is CORRECT?   48.____

    A. All children who have rheumatic fever will have heart disease.
    B. Some children who have had rheumatic fever will have heart disease.
    C. No children who have had rheumatic fever will have heart disease.
    D. All children with heart disease have had rheumatic fever.

49. Of the following, which orthopedic disability gives rise to special educational placement of the LARGEST number of children?   49.____

    A. Slipped epiphysis   B. Multiple sclerosis
    C. Lordosis   D. Otitis

50. A disease in which the muscles appear to be replaced with fatty tissue is   50.____

    A. epiphysitis   B. kyphosis
    C. muscular dystrophy   D. Still's disease

KEY (CORRECT ANSWERS)

1. C	11. A	21. A	31. B	41. B
2. D	12. B	22. A	32. A	42. B
3. D	13. A	23. B	33. C	43. B
4. D	14. A	24. D	34. D	44. A
5. B	15. A	25. B	35. D	45. D
6. A	16. B	26. D	36. C	46. D
7. D	17. A	27. A	37. B	47. B
8. C	18. A	28. D	38. B	48. B
9. A	19. B	29. D	39. A	49. A
10. C	20. B	30. A	40. A	50. C

EXAMINATION SECTION
TEST 1

DIRECTIONS: Each question or incomplete statement is followed by several suggested answers or completions. Select the one that BEST answers the question or completes the statement. *PRINT THE LETTER OF THE CORRECT ANSWER IN THE SPACE AT THE RIGHT.*

1. Natural resistance is lowered MOST by

    A. fatigue   B. reduction diet
    C. cold diet   D. lack of immunization

1.____

2. Cirrhosis of the liver is USUALLY caused by

    A. bacterial contamination of food
    B. a virus
    C. excessive use of highly seasoned foods
    D. extreme malnutrition

2.____

3. The true carriers of heredity are

    A. neurons   B. chromosomes
    C. sex cells   D. genes

3.____

4. The MOST serious form of food poisoning is

    A. undulant fever   B. botulism
    C. bacterial contamination   D. trichinosis

4.____

5. The filtering device of the kidneys is the

    A. glomerulus   B. jejunum
    C. ileum   D. nephron

5.____

6. MOST commonly affected by arteriosclerosis are the

    A. lungs   B. kidneys   C. nerves   D. senses

6.____

7. The Schick test indicates immunity to

    A. diphtheria   B. smallpox
    C. tetanus   D. tuberculosis

7.____

8. Difficulty in speaking is known as

    A. axphyxia   B. aphasia   C. amnesia   D. anorexia

8.____

9. Heat destroys bacteria by

    A. enucleation
    B. hemolysis
    C. coagulating protein
    D. making the cell wall permeable

9.____

10. The value of antihistaminic compounds lies PRIMARILY in their ability to   10._____

    A. increase intervals between infections
    B. relieve allergic manifestations
    C. immunize
    D. prevent the spread of infection

11. A *stroke* may be caused by   11._____

    A. cerebral hemorrhage   B. caecal dilation
    C. aortal thrombosis   D. pleural edema

12. The control of automatic breathing is located in the   12._____

    A. cerebrum   B. cerebellum
    C. spinal cord   D. medulla oblongata

13. Overweight people have less   13._____

    A. need for relaxation   B. resistance to infection
    C. danger of heart disease   D. inclination to diabetes

14. Rheumatic fever is associated with   14._____

    A. infections caused by the hemolytic streptococcus
    B. violent injury to one of the limbs
    C. viral infections of the respiratory tract
    D. bacterial infections of the bones

15. Active immunity is acquired through   15._____

    A. production of antibodies
    B. imperviousness of skin tissue
    C. enzyme activity
    D. washing action of mucous membranes

16. The value of antihistaminic compounds lies PRIMARILY in their ability to relieve the   16._____
effects of

    A. allergies   B. immunization
    C. infections   D. nausea

17. The purpose of vaccines is to   17._____

    A. reduce the causative organism
    B. develop scar tissue
    C. stimulate growth of antibodies
    D. produce bacteriostasis

18. Hepatitis is a disease of the   18._____

    A. renals   B. spleen   C. liver   D. pancreas

19. Salk serum is administered to prevent   19._____

    A. measles   B. diphtheria
    C. poliomyelitis   D. whooping cough

20. Cancer of the blood is 20.____

    A. carcinoma   B. sarcoma
    C. leukemia   D. epithelioma

21. Pellagra indicates a deficiency of 21.____

    A. ascorbic acid   B. niacin
    C. thiamine   D. riboflavin

22. Goiters are caused by lack of 22.____

    A. iodine in the food
    B. iron in food
    C. chlorine in the water supply
    D. vitamins in vegetables

23. The MOST frequent cause of death in the United States today is 23.____

    A. cancer   B. tuberculosis
    C. poliomyelitis   D. heart ailments

24. Average adult temperature by rectum is 24.____

    A. 99.6   B. 97.6   C. 98.6   D. 100.6

25. Metaplasia refers to disturbances of the 25.____

    A. mucous membranes   B. epithelial tissues
    C. cartilage   D. basal metabolism

26. The blood group which is commonly referred to as the *universal recipient* is 26.____

    A. A   B. B   C. AB   D. O

27. A contagious disease of the conjunctiva is 27.____

    A. glaucoma   B. xeropthalmia
    C. trachoma   D. hyperopia

28. Gamma globulins used in the protection against measles and polio contain 28.____

    A. toxoids   B. dead viruses
    C. weakened viruses   D. antibodies

29. A set of symptoms which usually occur together is known as the 29.____

    A. syndrome   B. prognosis   C. synedoche   D. prolan

30. Slow-acting penicillin controls the incidence of 30.____

    A. pneumonia   B. gonorrhea
    C. meningitis   D. measles

31. Vaccine is a 31.____

    A. cure   B. preventive
    C. remedy   D. stimulant

32. MOST commonly affected by arteriosclerosis are the   32._____

    A. kidneys   B. lungs   C. heart   D. brain

33. A nervous disorder characterized by involuntary action of the muscles which sometimes   33._____
    accompanies rheumatic fever is referred to as

    A. cerebral palsy   B. chorea
    C. neuralgia   D. arthritis

34. When edema is present, sodium intake is restricted because it   34._____

    A. slows the heartbeat
    B. causes hardening of the arteries
    C. increases urinary output
    D. holds fluid in the tissues

35. Leukemia is   35._____

    A. characterized by an increase in red blood cells
    B. a malignant disease
    C. a disease of the blood vessels
    D. always fatal within six months from the onset of symptoms

36. The child with mumps MUST be considered to be a source of contagion until   36._____

    A. his temperature returns to normal
    B. at least four weeks have elapsed since the onset of symptoms
    C. all swelling disappears
    D. the rash has disappeared completely

37. Infectious hepatitis may be transmitted by the patient   37._____

    A. for as long as two months after the onset of symptoms
    B. only for the first few days of the illness
    C. until he receives an injection of gamma globulin
    D. only until after the jaundice is no longer noticeable

38. The American Red Cross was founded by   38._____

    A. Florence Nightingale   B. Clara Barton
    C. Ellen Richards   D. Anton Leeuwenholk

39. The Schick test is used to determine susceptibility to   39._____

    A. poliomyelitis   B. scarlet fever
    C. diphtheria   D. typhoid fever

40. Glorieruli, which help remove impurities from the blood, are found in the   40._____

    A. liver   B. gall bladder
    C. lungs   D. kidneys

41. All of the following pertain to skin diseases EXCEPT   41._____

    A. glossitis   B. impetigo   C. herpes   D. cheilitis

42. A drug commonly used to treat bronchial infections is   42._____

    A. heroin   B. codeine   C. cocaine   D. morphine

43. The relationship between the incidence of cancer and smoking is   43._____

    A. inconclusive   B. negative
    C. positive   D. slightly negative

44. Due to advances in immunization, each of the following communicable childhood dis-   44._____
eases are rarely found in the United States EXCEPT

    A. diphtheria   B. measles
    C. polio   D. chickenpox

45. A child in the acute stage of rheumatic fever should be given   45._____

    A. liquids only
    B. only two meals a day
    C. double servings rich in calories
    D. small frequent feedings

KEY (CORRECT ANSWERS)

1.	A	11.	A	21.	B	31.	B	41.	A
2.	D	12.	D	22.	A	32.	A	42.	B
3.	D	13.	B	23.	D	33.	B	43.	C
4.	B	14.	A	24.	C	34.	D	44.	D
5.	A	15.	A	25.	C	35.	B	45.	D
6.	B	16.	A	26.	C	36.	C		
7.	A	17.	C	27.	C	37.	A		
8.	B	18.	C	28.	D	38.	B		
9.	C	19.	C	29.	A	39.	C		
10.	B	20.	C	30.	B	40.	D		

TEST 2

Each question or incomplete statement is followed by several suggested answers or completions. Select the one that BEST answers the question or completes the statement. *PRINT THE LETTER OF THE CORRECT ANSWER IN THE SPACE AT THE RIGHT.*

1. A malignant disease of the bone marrow is   1.____

   A. leukemia   B. cirrhosis
   C. osteoporosis   D. nephrosis

2. Dyspnea means difficult   2.____

   A. and labored breathing
   B. discharge of urine
   C. or deranged digestion
   D. pronouncing of vocal sounds

3. Underactivity of the thyroid gland in infants may produce the condition known as   3.____

   A. gigantism   B. Addison's disease
   C. exophthalmic goiter   D. cretinism

4. The number of chromosomes which a person inherits from each of his parents is   4.____

   A. 24   B. 35   C. 48   D. 12

5. The four diseases against which an infant should be immunized are smallpox, diphtheria,   5.____
   whooping cough, and

   A. measles   B. tetanus
   C. mumps   D. scarlet fever

6. A disease characterized by tender bleeding gums, swollen painful joints, and weakened   6.____
   muscles is

   A. scurvy   B. anemia   C. diabetes   D. carcinoma

7. Of the following diseases, the one that is NOT directly attributable to a specific vitamin   7.____
   deficiency is

   A. scurvy   B. tularemia   C. pellagra   D. rickets

8. A magenta-colored tongue is a symptom indicating a lack of sufficient   8.____

   A. vitamin A   B. thiamine
   C. niacin   D. riboflavin

9. Diabetic coma is caused by   9.____

   A. too much sugar in the diet
   B. too little food intake
   C. imperfect utilization of fat
   D. an overdose of insulin

10. An example of a non-contagious infection is   10.____

    A. tetanus   B. measles
    C. hepatitis   D. smallpox

11. Infection or irritation of small pouches located along the walls of the small intestines   11.____
results in a condition called

    A. diverticulitis   B. nephritis
    C. gastritis   D. glossitis

12. PKU, a disease in which phenylalanine accumulates in the body, due to faulty metabo-   12.____
lism, results in

    A. bone softening in adults
    B. hardening of the corneal tissues
    C. capillary fragility
    D. mental retardation in children

13. Penicillin spores   13.____

    A. are present in the air in Northern Alaska
    B. are destroyed by cold storage for two years
    C. germinate in bright sunlight
    D. develop rapidly in dry atmosphere at 30° F

14. Albino rats are used experimentally to determine vitamin C deficiency because   14.____

    A. they are allergic to scurvy
    B. they are capable of manufacturing their own ascorbic acid
    C. the symptoms shown do not parallel those in human beings
    D. the effects shown are not clear enough for observation

15. Kyphosis is a term used to designate   15.____

    A. angular curvature of the spine
    B. dryness of the mucous membrane
    C. fissures of extreme corners of the mouth
    D. scaly scalp condition

16. The first man to attribute the cause of beri-beri to dietary origin was   16.____

    A. Takaki   B. Eijkman   C. Funk   D. Lavoisier

17. An outstanding characteristic of the aging process is   17.____

    A. unfavorable reaction to stress
    B. lack of self-reliance
    C. increased irritability
    D. increased heart activity

18. The disease that can be transmitted to human beings by infected rabbits is   18.____

    A. undulant fever   B. tularemia
    C. trichinosis   D. trichinella

19. All of the following are correct associations EXCEPT 19.____

    A. Salk - dead polio vaccine
    B. Sabin - live polio vaccine
    C. Samos - weather satellite
    D. Shepard - suborbital space flight

20. Herpes simplex is an inflammation which affects the 20.____

    A. hair   B. skin   C. bones   D. toenails

21. Of the following diseases, the one USUALLY spread by rats and fleas is 21.____

    A. typhoid fever   B. sleeping sickness
    C. cholera   D. bubonic plague

22. Of the following, the treatment which would have a diuretic effect is 22.____

    A. liquid intake   B. enema
    C. dilantin sodium   D. fluorides

23. Inflammation of the membranes covering the lungs and lining the chest cavity is called 23.____

    A. asthma   B. laryngitis
    C. sinusitis   D. pleurisy

24. Hardening of the eyeball, which may lead to blindness in middle-aged or elderly persons, is known as 24.____

    A. conjunctivitis   B. trachoma
    C. glaucoma   D. cataract

25. The artery MOST commonly used to count the pulse is the 25.____

    A. temporal   B. carotid   C. radial   D. femoral

26. MOST cases of obesity in this country result from 26.____

    A. overeating   B. glandular imbalance
    C. heredity   D. economic affluence

27. Observable evidence of vitamin A deficiency in children is 27.____

    A. inflammation of eyelids
    B. magenta-colored tongue
    C. sores at angles of lips
    D. coarse, brittle, lusterless hair

28. Cryogenic surgery is a freezing method used in the treatment of 28.____

    A. Parkinson's disease   B. xerophthalmia
    C. diabetes   D. pellagra

29. A deficiency of niacin USUALLY results in 29.____

    A. osteomalacia   B. rickets
    C. caries   D. pellagra

30. A vaccine is introduced into the body to

    A. develop scar tissue
    B. produce bacteriostasis
    C. stimulate growth of specific antibodies
    D. reduce the causative organism

30._____

31. The value of anti-histaminic compounds lies PRIMARILY in their ability to relieve the effects of

    A. athetosis   B. infections
    C. nausea   D. allergies

31._____

32. The danger of strontium 90 lies in the fact that it

    A. is ultimately concentrated in bone tissue
    B. causes tumors in smooth muscle tissue
    C. is absorbed by the soil
    D. renders the atmosphere unfit for breathing

32._____

33. The effect of morphine which is believed to encourage addiction is the

    A. drowsiness, sleep, and dreams
    B. exaggerated feeling of well-being
    C. relief from pain
    D. dulling of perception

33._____

34. Ultraviolet rays harm the eyes by

    A. spotting the cornea
    B. enlarging the pupil
    C. destroying the visual purple
    D. drying the retina

34._____

35. Cortisone is used to relieve the symptoms of

    A. mental disorders   B. arthritis
    C. diabetes   D. heart disease

35._____

36. Pigeon-chest, joint enlargements, beaded ribs, and soft bones are symptoms of

    A. beri-beri   B. rickets   C. scurvy   D. pellagra

36._____

37. A fatty liver caused by prolonged use of alcohol

    A. raises the riboflavin requirement
    B. delays energy production
    C. contributes to development of cirrhosis
    D. speeds up liver action

37._____

38. The deficiency disease associated with ascorbic acid is

    A. beri-beri   B. scurvy
    C. rickets   D. night blindness

38._____

39. The process by which vital arteries become clogged or narrowed is

39.____

    A. atherosclerosis   B. thrombosis
    C. cirrhosis   D. scoliosis

40. Artery deposits in atherosclerosis are partially formed by

40.____

    A. cholesterol   B. glycerol
    C. stereols   D. glycols

41. Heart attacks are MORE common in adults

41.____

    A. who are obese   B. with lung infections
    C. who are underweight   D. with abdominal injuries

42. Vitamin A deficiency is associated with

42.____

    A. keratitis   B. scurvy
    C. capillary fragility   D. osteomalacia

43. Vitamin B deficiency is associated with all of the following EXCEPT

43.____

    A. blood clotting   B. pellagra
    C. polyneuritis   D. anorexia

44. The treatment of alcoholic pellagra is

44.____

    A. a balanced diet
    B. oral antibiotics
    C. thiamin injections with an adequate diet
    D. penicillin injections with a balanced diet

45. Aureomycin was developed by

45.____

    A. Fleming   B. Waksman   C. Banting   D. Duggar

KEY (CORRECT ANSWERS)

1. A	11. A	21. C	31. D	41. A
2. A	12. D	22. A	32. A	42. A
3. D	13. A	23. D	33. B	43. A
4. A	14. C	24. C	34. C	44. C
5. B	15. A	25. C	35. B	45. D
6. A	16. B	26. A	36. B	
7. B	17. A	27. D	37. C	
8. D	18. B	28. A	38. B	
9. C	19. C	29. D	39. A	
10. A	20. B	30. C	40. A	

EXAMINATION SECTION
TEST 1

DIRECTIONS: Each question or incomplete statement is followed by several suggested answers or completions. Select the one that BEST answers the question or completes the statement. *PRINT THE LETTER OF THE CORRECT ANSWER IN THE SPACE AT THE RIGHT.*

1. The *preferred* method of controlling hemorrhage is by   1.____

    A. applying pressure at the pressure points
    B. using a wide elastic tourniquet
    C. applying pressure over the wound with a clean cloth
    D. applying a large gauze dressing to absorb and clot the blood

2. For general use, the BEST method of artificial respiration is   2.____

    A. back pressure - arm lift
    B. breathe into mouth of the victim
    C. prone - pressure
    D. compression - release

3. For an adult with a normal skin, the temperature of the hot water bottle should be *between*   3.____

    A. 120°-130° F.   B. 100°-110° F.
    C. 140°-150° F.   D. 160°-170° F.

4. Penicillin was discovered by   4.____

    A. Jonas Salk   B. Alexander Fleming
    C. R. J. Diebos   D. Selman A. Waksman

5. Underweight is the PRIMARY contributory factor in   5.____

    A. still birth   B. premature labor
    C. anomalies in the birth process   D. abnormal deliveries

6. The part of the brain that is associated with memory is the   6.____

    A. cerebellum   B. pons varolii
    C. medulla oblongata   D. cerebrum

7. To restore the markings on a mouth thermometer,   7.____

    A. dip the thermometer in melted wax
    B. apply sealing wax and scrape off excess
    C. apply dark red nail polish and wife off at once
    D. dip in eosin solution and wipe off

8. The compound which is NOT a constituent of normal urine is   8.____

    A. ammonia   B. creatinine
    C. hippuric acid   D. indican

9. A water solution of ammonia is a(n)   9._____

   A. acid   B. basic salt   C. base   D. acid salt

10. The substance that is NOT used in testing for sugar is   10._____

   A. clinitest   B. phenolsulphonephthalein
   C. Fehling's solution   D. Benedict's solution

11. The substances that are NOT miscible are   11._____

   A. olive oil and acetic acid
   B. glycerine and alcohol
   C. soap and water
   D. linseed oil and lime-water

12. The downward pressure of the water in an enema can depend upon the   12._____

   A. speed of flow
   B. size of the tube opening
   C. quantity of fluid used
   D. the height of the surface of the water above the patient

13. The administration of vaccine should   13._____

   A. precede exposure to the disease
   B. reduce the duration of the disease
   C. follow after the disease has run its course
   D. prevent further spread of the infection

14. The SAFEST way of dusting a sick room is with a   14._____

   A. vacuum machine   B. feather duster
   C. damp cloth   D. dry cloth

15. *Before* disposing of food that is left over on a tray of a patient with a communicable dis-   15._____
ease, it should be

   A. wrapped in newspaper   B. boiled for 5 minutes
   C. boiled for 10 minutes   D. boiled for 15 minutes

16. A sheet which is stained by body discharges should FIRST be   16._____

   A. bleached   B. washed with warm water and soap
   C. boiled   D. rinsed in cold water

17. The ill person should be kept warm because in this way the blood   17._____

   A. *increases* in viscosity   B. *decreases* in viscosity
   C. *decreases* in fluidity   D. *increases* in saline cotent

18. Longer-acting penicillin has been an *effective* influence in the control of   18._____

   A. gonorrhea   B. tuberculosis   C. meningitis   D. measles

19. A stimulant for the respiratory center is   19._____

   A. carbon dioxide   B. ethyl chloride
   C. oxygen   D. nitrous oxide

20. The parts of the nervous system stimulated by strychnine are the   20._____

     A. hepatic and renal nerves
     B. brain and spinal cord
     C. autonomic ganglia and sciatic nerves
     D. coronary and pulmonary nerves

21. The GREATEST disease threat to the newborn in the United States is   21._____

     A. scarlet fever   B. diarrhea
     C. whooping cough   D. measles

22. To keep MOST cut flowers fresh,   22._____

     A. cut the end slantwise with a sharp knife
     B. cut the stems when they wilt, using scissors
     C. change the water every day
     D. use very cold water

23. Solutions are absorbed MORE rapidly when   23._____

     A. they are in concentrated form
     B. they are slightly diluted
     C. spread over a large surface
     D. spread over a limited area

24. Natural resistance to infection is *lowered* by   24._____

     A. fatigue   B. reducing diets
     C. cold weather   D. lack of immunization

25. Diphtheria can be prevented through the use of   25._____

     A. the Schick test   B. diphtheria toxoid
     C. therapeutic antiserum   D. antibiotics

KEY (CORRECT ANSWERS)

1.	C		11.	A
2.	B		12.	D
3.	A		13.	A
4.	B		14.	C
5.	B		15.	B
6.	D		16.	D
7.	C		17.	B
8.	D		18.	A
9.	C		19.	A
10.	B		20.	B

21.	B
22.	A
23.	C
24.	A
25.	B

——————

TEST 2

DIRECTIONS: Each question or incomplete statement is followed by several suggested answers or completions. Select the one that BEST answers the question or completes the statement. *PRINT THE LETTER OF THE CORRECT ANSWER IN THE SPACE AT THE RIGHT.*

1. Audible sound is measured in terms of

   A. farads   B. decibels   C. ohms   D. rels

1.____

2. Reduction in incidental nausea during pregnancy has been effected by an increase in the intake of

   A. ascorbic acid   B. vitamin D
   C. vitamin B-complex   D. minerals

2.____

3. Diet therapy is concerned *principally* with

   A. stimulation of impaired tissues
   B. maintaining health
   C. modification of customary diet
   D. reducing caloric intake

3.____

4. *Most* economic for protein re-enforcement of the diet is

   A. egg yolk   B. ice cream
   C. cream cheese   D. skim-milk powder

4.____

5. When putting drops in the eyes, place them

   A. under the upper eyelid
   B. on the inside of lower eyelid
   C. in the aqueous chamber
   D. on the iris

5.____

6. The MOST effective control of the spread of tuberculosis relies on

   A. vaccine   B. case finding
   C. Mantoux test   D. diet and rest

6.____

7. The effect of below-freezing temperatures on microbes is to

   A. destroy the pathogens   B. kill them
   C. stimulate sporification   D. check growth and multiplication

7.____

8. An anodyne

   A. is an antidote
   B. is an antiseptic
   C. prolongs the life of red blood corpuscles
   D. relieves pain

8.____

9. Boiling an article in water for 10 minutes will destroy

   A. pathogens   B. non-spore-forming microbes
   C. spore-forming microbes   D. spore-forming patgens

9.____

10. An *inexpensive* disinfectant is   10.____

    A.   bichloride of mercury
    B.   potassium permanganate
    C.   creosote
    D.   alcohol

11. The source of infection MOST difficult to control is   11.____

    A.   water   B.   insects   C.   food   D.   air

12. Pasteurization of milk   12.____

    A.   kills pathogenic bacteria
    B.   destroys bacteria of all kinds
    C.   controls the growth of bacteria   D.   sterilizes milk

13. The COMMONEST cause of apoplexy is   13.____

    A.   coronary thrombosis and arterial dilation
    B.   hardening of the arteries and hypertension
    C.   emotional shock and low blood pressure
    D.   uremia and aphasia

14. Poor diet influences MOST the occurrence of   14.____

    A.   metabolic diseases   B.   cancer
    C.   nephritis   D.   hypertension

15. In proper handwashing, be sure to use   15.____

    A.   cold water   B.   soap, water and adequate friction
    C.   liquid soap   D.   very hot water

16. At present, antibiotics are recognized to be   16.____

    A.   a factor in altering the natural germ balance in the body
    B.   ineffective in developing toxic reactions
    C.   ineffective in developing allergic reactions
    D.   most desirable in fixed antibiotic combinaations

17. The study of pathogenic organisms in relation to disease is the science of 17.____

    A.   microbiology   B.   blocking therapy
    C.   chemotherapy   D.   replacement therapy

18. Atoms of an element that differ in atomic weight are called   18.____

    A.   molecules   B.   neutrons   C.   isotopes   D.   particles

19. The *danger* of strontium 90 lies in the fact that it   19.____

    A.   is absorbed and concentrated in bone tissue
    B.   causes tumors in smooth muscles
    C.   falls back and is absorbed by the soil near the explosion
    D.   renders the atmosphere unfit for breathing

20. A vaccine is introduced into the body to   20._____

    A. kill the causative organism
    B. stimulate growth of specific antibodies
    C. inhibit growth of the causative organism
    D. produce bacteriostasis

21. The *preventive* treatment for diphtheria consists of injections of   21._____

    A. gamma globulin   B. pertussis
    C. toxoid   D. convalescent serum

22. Gamma globulin *usually* gives temporary immunity after exposure to   22._____

    A. whooping cough   B. mumps
    C. measles   D. chicken pox

23. The substance among the following which is an *immunizing* serum is   23._____

    A. diphtheria antitoxin   B. tubercle bacilli
    C. gamma globulin
    D. BCG (bacillus Calmette-Guerin)

24. The "confection" for pre-school children approved by the American Dental Society is   24._____

    A. non-sweet soft drinks   B. hard candies
    C. raw fruit   D. crisp cookies and crackers

25. The effect of morphine which MOST encourages to addiction is   25._____

    A. sensing an exaggerated feeling of well
        being
    B. the dulling of perception
    C. drowsiness, sleep and dreams
    D. relief from pain

KEY (CORRECT ANSWERS)

1.	B		11.	D
2.	C		12.	A
3.	C		13.	B
4.	D		14.	A
5.	B		15.	B
6.	B		16.	A
7.	D		17.	A
8.	D		18.	C
9.	B		19.	A
10.	C		20.	B

21.	C
22.	C
23.	B
24.	C
25.	A

———

TEST 3

DIRECTIONS: Each question or incomplete statement is followed by several suggested answers or completions. Select the one that BEST answers the question or completes the statement. *PRINT THE LETTER OF THE CORRECT ANSWER IN THE SPACE AT THE RIGHT.*

1. In preparing a patient for hospital care, it would be MOST advisable for the nurse to tell the patient

    1._____

    A. the length of time he will probably have to stay for complete recovery
    B. that the term "bed rest" means that he will have bathroom privileges
    C. that the best form of therapy for him may be bed rest without medication or surgery
    D. that the hospital is a very fine place, that the food is excellent and that he will enjoy the routine

2. Of the following symptoms, the one which would be *least likely* to cause a person to consult a physician for chest examination is

    2._____

    A. continuous loss of weight
    B. a cough lasting longer than three weeks
    C. a slight elevation of temperature in the afternoon
    D. fresh blood in the stools

3. The PRIMARY purpose of a cancer detection center is to

    3._____

    A. examine, for diagnosis, persons who are suspected of having cancer
    B. examine people who are presumably healthy
    C. treat people who have a diagnosis of cancer
    D. follow-up patients who have had cancer and are apparently cured

4. Addition of fluorine to drinking water which has a low fluorine level has PRIMARILY the effect of aiding in the

    4._____

    A. strengthening of bones
    B. improving of skin texture
    C. preventing of dental caries
    D. preventing of scurvy

5. The LEADING cause of death in the 5- to 14-year age group is

    5._____

    A. pneumonia   B. accidents
    C. rheumatic fever   D. scarlet fever

6. The drug which has given new hope to victims of arthritis is

    6._____

    A. ACTH   B. histamine   C. penicillin   D. chloromycetin

7. The one of the following which is the leading cause of death is

    7._____

    A. tuberculosis   B. diseases of the heart
    C. cancer   D. accidents

8. Robert Koch is known for his identification of

    8._____

    A. tubercle bacilli   B. diphtheria bacilli
    C. treponema-pallidum organism   D. Neisseria gonorrhoeae

9. The BEST definition for *myopia* is 9.____

    A. near-sightedness   B. far-sightedness
    C. cross eyes   D. blocking of the lacrimal duct

10. Of the following, the one which represents *normal* vision is 10.____

    A. 20/200   B. 20/30   C. 20/20   D. 15/30

11. Of the following statements, the one which is MOST accurate is that 11.____

    A. to prevent trichinosis, it is necessary to roast beef and lamb until well done
    B. brucellosis is developed in humans only when they drink milk containing the bru-
cellosis organism
    C. because of the possibility of infection by the rabies organism it is necessary that all
breaks in the skin caused by the bite of a dog receive immediate medical attention
and be reported to the police
    D. because the staphylococcus organisms multiply most readily in a temperature
below $50°$ Fahrenheit, it is safe to keep custard-filled pastry indefinitely at room
temperature of $68°$ Fahrenheit

12. Of the following definitions, the one which is CORRECT is that the 12.____

    A. infant mortality rate is the number of deaths of infants under one year of age per
1000 live births
    B. maternal mortality rate is the number of deaths from puerperal causes per 10,000
population
    C. morbidity rate is the number of deaths per 1000 population
    D. neonatal mortality rate is the number of deaths of infants under one week of age

13. Of the following, the one which is NOT a sign of pregnancy in the first trimester is 13.____

    A. absence of menses   B. marked changes in breasts
    C. nausea in the morning   D. feeling of fetal movements

14. The hazards of childbearing vary with the health or disease of the individual. 14.____
Of the following conditions, the one which is NOT usually considered a childbearing
hazard is

    A. tuberculosis
    B. nephritis
    C. diseases of the heart
    D. poliomyelitis involving lower extremities only

15. Of the following statements concerning poliomyelitis, the one that is CORRECT is that 15.____

    A. poliomyelitis is a disease with initial symptoms of an upper respiratory infection and
cough
    B. in the care of the acute poliomyelitis case it is important to handle the affected limb
at the insertion and origin of the muscle only
    C. poliomyelitis, in the acute stages, may affect the spine. It is important, therefore,
that the patient be kept on a soft mattress
    D. if the poliomyelitis victim has a marked weakness of certain muscles two months
after onset, there is no hope for further improvement

16. A nurse working with children should know that, of the following statements, the only CORRECT one is that   16._____

    A. Koplik spots in the mucous membrane of the mouth are an early symptom of measles
    B. a strawberry tongue is found in chicken-pox
    C. enlargement of and pain in the parotid glands are early manifestations of scarlet fever
    D. large blisters, first appearing on exposed surfaces, are characteristic of German measles

17. Of the following types of growths, the one which is a *benign* tumor is   17._____

    A. adenoma   B. carcinoma   C. sarcoma   D. neuroblastoma

18. A nurse should know that, of the following statements, the CORRECT one is that   18._____

    A. one average serving of dark cereal furnishes the necessary requirement of iron for an adolescent girl for one day
    B. one quart of milk furnishes the necessary calcium requirement of a pregnant woman for one day
    C. bananas are a very rich source of vitamin A
    D. glandular meats, sugars, and cereals are good sources of vitamin C

19. Of the following foods, the one RICHEST in thiamine is   19._____

    A. oranges   B. liver
    C. yellow vegetables   D. eggs

20. Of the following diseases, the one NOT caused by a lack of essential food elements is   20._____

    A. rickets   B. scurvy   C. beriberi   D. tetanus

21. Of the following explanations, the BEST one that a nurse can give to a mother who complains that her 15-year-old adolescent boy has a huge appetite is that the   21._____

    A. boy may gain 20 pounds in a year and 4 to 6 inches in height; also, that if he is active in sports, he may need up to 4000 calories daily
    B. boy is under a great deal of nervous tension, and that, therefore, he eats huge amounts to satisfy this desire to be "doing something"
    C. boy is in danger of becoming excessively heavy, and that, therefore, his diet should be restricted by limiting milk and meats
    D. boy's diet should be restricted by reducing amounts of all food taken until his weight is 10% below the average

22. With respect to obesity and diet, the LEAST acceptable statement of the following is that   22._____

    A. obesity constitutes a public health problem of importance, since obese persons are more apt to develop diabetes and degenerative diseases
    B. obesity usually results from an habitual intake of more food than the energy output requires
    C. the treatment of obesity should involve re-education of the appetite
    D. the recommended intake for an obese person is 3000 calories daily, since the diet should be adequate in respect to all essential nutrients

23. Diseases associated with the aged are assuming increasing importance. 23._____
One of these chronic conditions, the nurse frequently finds, is acute cerebral thrombosis with resulting hemiplegia. To bring about *maximum* rehabilitation, the nurse should assist in a program in which

   A. the patient is encouraged to help himself only when, and if, he feels he is able to do so
   B. the patient is immobilized until the acute phase is over and the patient is able to start to help himself
   C. any portion of the body is prevented from remaining in a position of flexion long enough to permit muscle shortening to occur
   D. the use of the affected muscles and the opposing muscles is discouraged for at least four weeks following the onset of illness

24. The nurse should know that the age period during which there is the LARGEST incidence of rheumatic fever is from 24._____

   A. birth to five years   B. six to twelve years
   C. fourteen to twenty years
   D. twenty-one to twenty-six years

25. A lateral curvature of the spine is known as 25._____

   A. scoliosis   B. lordosis   C. kyphosis   D. trichinosis

_____

KEYS (CORRECT ANSWERS)

1.	C	11.	C
2.	D	12.	A
3.	B	13.	D
4.	C	14.	D
5.	B	15.	B
6.	A	16.	A
7.	B	17.	A
8.	A	18.	B
9.	A	19.	B
10.	C	20.	D

21.	A
22.	D
23.	C
24.	B
25.	A

_____

TEST 4

DIRECTIONS: Each question or incomplete statement is followed by several suggested answers or completions. Select the one that BEST answers the question or completes the statement. *PRINT THE LETTER OF THE CORRECT ANSWER IN THE SPACE AT THE RIGHT.*

1. Cerebral palsy can BEST be described as a   1.____

    A. nerve infection which causes the incoordination of the muscles
    B. muscular deformity chiefly affecting the upper extremities
    C. neuro-muscular disability caused by injury to the motor centers of the brain
    D. muscular disfunction caused by injury to the spinal column

2. Of the following statements, the one which would be the MOST *inadvisable* for a nurse to tell diabetic patients is that   2.____

    A. it is advisable to see a doctor at regular intervals
    B. extreme cleanliness is very important. Feet should be washed daily and skin kept soft
    C. as gangrene may develop in older diabetics from simple bruises or breaks in the skin, all injuries should be treated immediately
    D. in giving foot care, the nails should be cut as short as possible and the cuticle removed by cutting

3. Of the following definitions, the one which is BEST is that   3.____

    A. pneumoperitoneum is the incision and drainage of the pleural space
    B. pneumolysis is an operation in which the infected lobe is removed
    C. pneumothorax is the introduction of air into the potential peritoneal cavity
    D. thoracoplasty is an operation in which parts of several ribs are removed to give a permanent collapse of the lung

4. With reference to tuberculosis, the one of the following statements which is INCORRECT is that   4.____

    A. the death rate from tuberculosis among men is approximately 50% higher than among women
    B. from birth until six months of age infants have an immunity to tuberculosis
    C. mortality from tuberculosis reaches its highest peak in men between the ages of 50 and 60
    D. the mortality rate for tuberculosis is very much lower in the elementary school age group than in all other groups

5. In counseling a person who has had tuberculosis, a nurse should suggest to him that,of the following types of work, the one which would be the MOST advisable for him to avoid is   5.____

    A. a job which requires rapid prolonged motions of the arms
    B. light assembly work in which the worker fits small parts together
    C. work in which the worker's value depends on delicacy of touch and close attention
    D. work which involves clerical, stenographic, or bookkeeping tasks

6. The age at which the average baby starts to creep is, *approximately,*   6._____

    A. 5 months   B. 9 months   C. 12 months   D. 14 months

7. Of the following statements, the one which is the MOST accurate is that   7._____

    A. a young baby begins to suck his thumb because he has not had enough sucking at breast or bottle to satisfy his sucking instinct
    B. diarrhea is a more frequent occurrence than constipation among very young babies that are bottle fed
    C. a baby weighing 6 to 8 pounds must be kept at a room temperature of 75 to 80° F ahrenheit, as his system for regulating body temperature has not been well developed
    D. a normal baby does not recognize a human face and does not respond to it until 4 to 5 months of age

8. In counseling a young mother of pre-school children, the one of the following which represents the MOST accurate statement is that   8._____

    A. by the age of two, a child is quite a social being; he is very easily satisfied and,in his emotional development , identifies himself with his parents
    B. between the ages of one and three years, an occasional temper tantrum merely means some frustrations that are normal; more frequent tantrums may indicate that the mother has not learned to handle the child tactfully
    C. at two and one half years of age, the frequent hitting of a playmate for taking toys, instead of asking for them, is abnormal and needs psychiatric guidance
    D. a two-year-old dresses himself, with the exception of tying shoe laces; he is toilet trained, and, if day wetting occurs, medical advice should be sought

9. On physical inspection of the young infant, the nurse looks for symptoms of brachial birth palsy.   9._____
   Of the following, the one which MOST accurately describes these symptoms is that

    A. the arm is limp at the side, the elbow is straight, and the forearm is pronated; inability to abduct, raise, and outwardly rotate the upper arm is noted
    B. the foot is twisted into a position of plantar flexion and inversion; this position raises the height of the longitudinal arch, causing a deformity
    C. there is a shortening of the leg, as the femoral head slides up along the sides of the ilium; abduction of the hip is limited
    D. the head is tipped to the side and twisted so that the chin points in the opposite direction

10. A nurse asked to appraise a home preparatory to discharge from the hospital of a premature baby, present weight 5 pounds, would NOT recommend that the baby be sent to this home at this time if   10._____

    A. the father has an income of $50 a week, and there are three young children
    B. the apartment is on the fourth floor, walk up; there are four rooms, of which two can be used as bedrooms
    C. one of the children was exposed to pertussis two weeks ago; he apparently has no symptoms
    D. the mother is under medical care for the treatment of nutritional anemia

11. A nurse should know that, of the following conditions, the one which is NOT a congenital   11.____
deformity is

    A. wryneck   B. club foot   C. spine bifida   D. kyphosis

12. A nurse should know that, with reference to the care of the premature infant, the one of   12.____
the following which is NOT indicated is

    A. the maintenance of normal body temperature
    B. proper feeding
    C. protection of the infant from exposure to infection
    D. removal from the incubator at least once a day for exercise

13. The term, "rooming in" program, refers to the program where the   13.____

    A. patient in labor is allowed to have her husband with her
    B. parents are advised to keep the infant in the sleeping room with them the first
        month of its life
    C. newborn is kept in the hospital room with the mother
    D. patient comes to the hospital five days prior to the expected delivery to become
        acquainted with the institution

14. The BEST advice you can give parents disturbed by their five-year-old child's habit of   14.____
nailbiting is to tell them to

    A. find out what some of the pressures on the child are and try to relieve them
    B. paint the child's fingers with the product "bitter aloes"
    C. point out to the child that this is a baby habit and not desirable in a school child
    D. punish the child by not allowing him to watch television or go to the movies

15. In certain periods of development, anti-social behavior in young children is considered   15.____
normal.
However, of the following situations, the one which merits referral to a mental hygiene
clinic is where a

    A. two-year-old persists in hitting his four-year-old brother
    B. three-year-old develops enuresis when a new baby is brought into the home
    C. four-year-old runs away from home at every opportunity
    D. six-year-old is not friendly, has no "pals" after six months in school, and participates
        in activities only when compelled to

16. Of the following, the one which is NOT in accord with accepted theories in child psychol-   16.____
ogy is that a young child should be

    A. comforted when he cries
    B. fed when he is hungry
    C. toilet trained when the mother feels it is necessary
    D. accepted as he is

17. With reference to syphilis, the one of the following statements which is CORRECT is that   17.____

    A. the incubation period is 10 to 90 days; average is 3 weeks
    B. the period of communicability is 2 weeks
    C. the mode of transmission is usually through indirect contact, as through towels and
        clothing
    D. methods of control include routine taking of blood pressure

18. Of the following statements concerning syphilis, the one which is MOST accurate is that   18.____

    A.   a positive blood test for syphilis always indicates that the patient is in an infectious state of the disease

    B.   when a pregnant woman with syphilis reports for treatment early in pregnancy and follows the doctor's orders throughout, there is very little danger of the baby being born with congenital syphilis

    C.   if the prescribed number of penicillin injections have been received by the patient with secondary syphilis, he will not be re-infected if exposed

    D.   the period between exposure and appearance of the first symptoms of syphilis is usually two to six days

19. The stage in which syphilis is usually NOT considered contagious is   19.____

    A.   primary   B.   secondary   C.   tertiary   D.   chancre

20. The incubation period of scarlet fever is   20.____

    A.   two to seven days   B.   seven to fourteen days
    C.   seven to twenty-one days   D.   fourteen to eighteendays

21. As a nurse you are frequently asked how to protect children against poliomyelitis. According to present teaching, the one of the following which you should NOT recommend is   21.____

    A.   avoiding groups and places of general assemblage where new contacts would be made

    B.   maintaining good personal and environment hygiene

    C.   avoiding chilling which lowers body resistance

    D.   exercising as much as possible, even to the point of tiring, in order to strengthen the body

22. Of the following diseases, the one characterized by "strawberry tongue" is   22.____

    A.   meningococcus meningitis   B.   poliomyelitis
    C.   German measles   D.   scarlet fever

23. Of the following statements concerning the transfer of communicable diseases from animal to man, the one which is CORRECT is that   23.____

    A.   tetanus is confined to persons who have eaten raw or insufficiently cooked meat, usually pork or pork product containing viable larvae

    B.   brucellosis is usually transmitted by house pets, such as parrots, canaries and pigeons

    C.   psittacosis is usually transmitted by cows, hogs, or goats

    D.   rickettsial pox is transmitted by common house mice, probably from mouse to man by a rodent mite

24. Of the following statements, the one which is CORRECT is that   24.____

    A.   Pasteur treatment is instituted to prevent the development of rabies

    B.   a smallpox epidemic may be prevented by rigid inspection of milk

    C.   hydrophobia is a synonym for tetanus

    D.   the feces and urine in cases of Vincent's agina should be disinfected

25. With reference to serum hepatitis (jaundice), the one of the following statements which is   25._____
CORRECT is that

  A. the virus causing it may be transmitted through parenteral inoculations of infected blood
  B. it has an incubation period of one to two months
  C. it is characterized by severe paroxysms of coughing, with little or no fever, and general muscle pains
  D. the victims do not receive immunizing agents or convalescent serum early enough

---

KEY (CORRECT ANSWERS)

1.	C	11.	D
2.	D	12.	D
3.	D	13.	C
4.	B	14.	A
5.	A	15.	D
6.	B	16.	C
7.	A	17.	A
8.	B	18.	B
9.	A	19.	C
10.	C	20.	A

21.	D
22.	D
23.	D
24.	A
25.	A

TEST 5

DIRECTIONS: Each question or incomplete statement is followed by several suggested answers or completions. Select the one that BEST answers the question or completes the statement. *PRINT THE LETTER OF THE CORRECT ANSWER IN THE SPACE AT THE RIGHT.*

1. Vitamin A is stored in the   1.____

   A. skeletal muscles   B. liver
   C. thyroid   D. brain

2. The MOST important single item of the diet is   2.____

   A. carbohydrates   B. water   C. milk   D. protein

3. The control of diabetes in children is   3.____

   A. more difficult than in adults   B. impossible
   C. relatively simple   D. not necessary

4. Obesity may be caused by   4.____

   A. lack of vitamins   B. excessive calorie intake
   C. gastronomy   D. high protein diet

5. Beriberi is caused by   5.____

   A. lack of thiamine   B. heredity
   C. faulty hygiene   D. a virus

6. Emotional disturbances   6.____

   A. hasten digestion   B. delay digestion
   C. cause uremia   D. result in loss of Vitamin B

7. Calorie is a   7.____

   A. unit of measurement   B. term used for digestibility
   C. need for nutrients   D. catalytic agent

8. A *substantial* source of iron is found in   8.____

   A. apricots   B. almonds   C. potatoes   D. cheese

9. Pasteurized milk is *valuable* in the diet because it is a good source of   9.____

   A. Vitamin K   B. amino acid   C. Vitamin B   D. rutin

10. Vitamin A helps to prevent   10.____

   A. night blindness   B. hemorrhage in newborn infant
   C. scurvy   D. destruction of connective tissue

11. In diarrhea, feed   11.____

   A. orange juice   B. boiled milk
   C. chopped spinach   D. stewed prunes

12. Swelling, heat and redness occur in an inflamed area because the capillaries become   12.____

    A. constricted   B. dilated
    C. ruptured   D. fenestrated

13. Bone owes its hardness CHIEFLY to the mineral salt   13.____

    A. calcium phosphorus   B. potassium iodide
    C. sodium carbonate   D. stearic acid

14. The number of vertebrae of the spinal column of a human is   14.____

    A. 33   B. 42   C. 28   D. 21

15. Sebaceous glands   15.____

    A. aid digestion   B. have ducts
    C. are attached to the muscles of the eye
    D. increase blood pressure

16. The audiometer is an instrument for measuring   16.____

    A. hearing acuity   B. vision accuracy
    C. temperature   D. pressure

17. Tic is a(n)   17.____

    A. poisonous product   B. insect
    C. connective tissue   D. twitching

18. Ringworm is caused by   18.____

    A. fungi   B. pediculi
    C. infection of the intestines D. impetigo

19. Mastoid is   19.____

    A. a woman who practices massage B. marasmus
    C. part of the temporal bone   D. inflammation of the breast

20. Morphology is a study of   20.____

    A. form   B. trench mouth   C. death   D. the fetus

21. The Rh factors are   21.____

    A. negative   B. positive
    C. negative and positive   D. none of these

22. Insomnia refers to   22.____

    A. unconsciousness   B. sleeplessness
    C. sleep walking   D. insensibility

23. Mortality refers to   23.____

    A. pulverization   B. death   C. motion   D. illness

24. Fungus is a
    A. form of plant life
    C. medication for inducing sleep
    B. division of a nucleus
    D. vitamin deficiency

24.____

25. The incubation period of the common cold is
    A. 27-36 hours   B. 7 days   C. 14 days   D. 21 days

25.____

KEY (CORRECT ANSWERS)

1. B	11. B
2. B	12. B
3. A	13. A
4. B	14. A
5. A	15. B
6. B	16. A
7. A	17. D
8. A	18. A
9. B	19. C
10. A	20. A

21. C
22. B
23. B
24. A
25. A

TEST 6

DIRECTIONS: Each question or incomplete statement is followed by several suggested answers or completions. Select the one that BEST answers the question or completes the statement. *PRINT THE LETTER OF THE CORRECT ANSWER IN THE SPACE AT THE RIGHT.*

1. Morphine addiction causes   1.____

   A. constriction of the pupil of the eye
   B. increase in heart rate   C. dilation of the cervix
   D. difficulty in hearing

2. Pigmentation   2.____

   A. depends upon the hemoglobin   B. reduces body heat
   C. protects tissues of the skin   D. produces color

3. In respiration,   3.____

   A. expiration is slower than inspiration
   B. receptors of the skin respond
   C. the hypothalmus is expanded
   D. enzymes are rendered inert

4. The permanent teeth in human adults should number   4.____

   A. 27   B. 32   C. 26   D. 34

5. The Newburgh-Kingston fluoridation experiment dealt with   5.____

   A. vitamin B in nutrition   B. anemia
   C. dental caries   D. malnutrition

6. The brain   6.____

   A. is dependent upon glucose for its energy
   B. functions in the final destruction of the red blood
   C. appears biconcave, is elastic and pliable
   D. separates the high pressure system of the arterial tree from the lower pressure
       system of the venous tree

7. Taste buds are located on the tongue *and*   7.____

   A. on the soft palate   B. at the Eustachian tube
   C. on posterior descending branch of the coronary
   D. in the atrium

8. Color blindness *sometimes* means   8.____

   A. hues of green and red are indistinguishable
   B. continuous winking when colors are dull
   C. disturbed equilibrium   D. irritated conjunctiva

9. Metabolism   9.____

   A. expresses the fact that nerve fibres give only one kind of reaction
   B. summarizes the activities each living cell must carry on

C. possesses the properties of irritability and conductivity
D. describes the membrane theory

10. The heat of the body is maintained by   10.____

A. oxidation   B. vertigo   C. gravity   D. hyperpnea

11. All cells   11.____

A. exist proximal to liquid environment
B. secrete a hormone which helps maintain the normal calcium level of the blood
C. differ in origin and function
D. are cone-shaped

12. Anoxia is   12.____

A. a colloidal solution that exerts pressure
B. plasma volume
C. body proteins
D. lack of oxygen

13. The heart rate   13.____

A. varies in individuals
B. increases from birth to old age
C. increases during first hours of sleep
D. decreases in hemorrhage

14. The heart begins to "beat"   14.____

A. immediately preceding birth
B. in the fetus at about the fourth week of fetal life
C. in the fetus during seventh month of fetal life
D. with the first cry after birth

15. A neuron consists of   15.____

A. fluid in the semicircular canals
B. conjugated protein which yields globin and hemin
C. a cell body and processes
D. a band of spectrum colors ranging from red to violet

16. The process of swallowing is called   16.____

A. delactation   B. diastasis   C. deglutition   D. emission

17. Histology   17.____

A. dissolves essential constituents in water
B. connects arterial and venous circulation
C. describes microscopic structure
D. reduces diseased structures

18. Prevent noise for the sick patient by

    A. removing the door hinges
    B. keeping the window shades rolled up
    C. padding the door latches
    D. repairing faucets

18.____

19. For the patient, select a room that is

    A. near the bathroom
    B. large enough for necessary furniture
    C. equipped with screened windows
    D. exposed to sunshine

19.____

20. Devices for elevating the patient's bed may be

    A. large books   B. kitchen chairs
    C. wooden bed-blocks   D. foot stools

20.____

21. A substitute for the rubber draw sheet is a(n)

    A. average sizedplastic dressercover
    B. old raincoat
    C. Sunday newspaper
    D. shower curtain

21.____

22. Prevent accidents due to poisons by

    A. labeling properly   B. storing outside of home
    C. substituting non-poisons D. destroying poisons

22.____

23. Most prone to accidents in the home is the

    A. young adult   B. middle-aged individual
    C. adolescent   D. aged individual

23.____

24. Mortality due to tuberculosis is rapidly declining through the use of

    A. tuberculin tests   B. preventive measures
    C. chemicals   D. statistics

24.____

25. A drug used in the treatment of mental illness is

    A. streptomycin   B. paramino-salicylic acid
    C. reserpine   D. cortisone

25.____

KEY (CORRECT ANSWERS)

1.	A		11.	A
2.	D		12.	D
3.	A		13.	A
4.	B		14.	B
5.	C		15.	C
6.	A		16.	C
7.	A		17.	C
8.	A		18.	C
9.	B		19.	A
10.	A		20.	C

21. D
22. A
23. D
24. C
25. C

TEST 7

DIRECTIONS: Each question or incomplete statement is followed by several suggested answers or completions. Select the one that BEST answers the question or completes the statement. *PRINT THE LETTER OF THE CORRECT ANSWER IN THE SPACE AT THE RIGHT.*

1. As a substitute for an emesis basin, use a(n)   1._____

    A. metal coffee can   B. small pyrex bowl
    C. old kitchen dish   D. small enamel sauce pan

2. To keep the feet of the patient in normal position,   2._____

    A. soak the feet   B. lubricate the feet
    C. use bed cradle   D. flex the ankles and toes

3. When using an aerosol bomb in the sick room,   3._____

    A. close the windows   B. remove the patient
    C. keep all food covered   D. follow-up with chlordane

4. When in doubt about the nature of a stain,   4._____

    A. swab with water   B. apply carbon tetrachloride
    C. consult professional cleaner D. saturate with kerosene

5. Flammable chemicals, if used in stain removal, should be used   5._____

    A. in a room   B. out-of-doors
    C. sparingly   D. with lint-free cloths

6. Paper supplies are used freely in the sick room since they are   6._____

    A. helpful in prevention   B. inexpensive
    C. clean   D. bright and colorful

7. Keep house pets out of the sickroom because they may   7._____

    A. be noisy   B. tire the patient
    C. carry disease elsewhere   D. jar furniture

8. Protect the top edge of the bed blanket from being soiled by   8._____

    A. folding the spread over it
    B. folding paper towels over it
    C. sewing a strip of muslin over it
    D. pinning a table napkin over it

9. Some nurses never become good housekeepers because they lack   9._____

    A. observation   B. interest   C. sensitivity   D. ability

10. When water is added to dry mustard, the reaction is   10._____

    A. polymerization   B. hydrolysis
    C. dehydration   D. neutralization

11. The efficacy of saline cathartics depends upon the   11.____

    A. selective action   B. osmotic pressure
    C. relaxation of smooth muscle   D. retarding of peristis

12. The chemical which stimulates the respiratory center is   12.____

    A. oxygen   B. carbon dioxide   C. calcium   D. nitrogen

13. Carbon dioxide and oxygen are exchanged in the air sacs by   13.____

    A. infusion   B. diffusion   C. reaction   D. filtration

14. The absorption of water through the intestinal wall is by   14.____

    A. filtration   B. osmosis   C. infiltration   D. fusion

15. Oils and water do not mix readily because of the difference in   15.____

    A. heat of fusion   B. surface tension
    C. heat of sublimation   D. freezing point

16. The lowering of the head, when a person feels faint, will increase the blood supply to the   16.____
    head by

    A. suction   B. gravity   C. siphonage   D. centripetalforce

17. The ventricles of the heart act like a   17.____

    A. lever   B. pump   C. siphon   D. barometer

18. Radon is radioactive gas which results when radium emits a(n)   18.____

    A. beta particle   B. alpha particle
    C. gamma ray   D. neutron

19. A rubber hot water bottle transfers heat to the skin CHIEFLY by   19.____

    A. conduction   B. convection   C. radiation   D. oxidation

20. A clinical thermometer is a(n)   20.____

    A. thermograph   B. maximum thermometer
    C. minimum thermometer   D. absolute thermometer

―――――――

KEY (CORRECT ANSWERS)

1.	A	11.	B
2.	C	12.	B
3.	B	13.	B
4.	C	14.	B
5.	B	15.	B
6.	A	16.	B
7.	C	17.	B
8.	C	18.	B
9.	D	19.	A
10.	B	20.	B

EXAMINATION SECTION
TEST 1

DIRECTIONS: Each question or incomplete statement is followed by several suggested answers or completions. Select the one that BEST answers the question or completes the statement. *PRINT THE LETTER OF THE CORRECT ANSWER IN THE SPACE AT THE RIGHT.*

1. The one of the following which is the MOST important requirement of a good menu is that it

    A. include a large variety of food
    B. list foods which are well-liked
    C. be printed neatly on a clean menu card
    D. be suited to the purpose for which it is planned

1.____

2. Of the following, the procedure which is MOST desirable for proper tray service is to

    A. heat all dishes before placing them on the tray
    B. serve hot food hot, and cold food cold
    C. have all patients elevated in order to permit easier swallowing of food
    D. always serve iced water on the tray

2.____

3. The PROPER position for the knife on the tray is

    A. above the dinner plate
    B. across the bread and butter plate
    C. to the right of the dinner plate
    D. next to the fork

3.____

4. For attractive tray service, it is MOST advisable to serve harvard beets

    A. on the plate with the meat
    B. in a small side vegetable dish
    C. on a bed of shredded lettuce
    D. with a very thick, heavy sauce

4.____

5. The kitchen dietitian can work MOST efficiently if her office is located

    A. away from the kitchen, so she can be free from distractions
    B. in a central position where she may view all that happens
    C. at the entrance to the kitchen where she can see people entering and leaving
    D. next to the pantry, so she can see that no unauthorized person enters

5.____

6. The PRIMARY purpose of keeping records in the dietary department is to

    A. reduce waste in ordering food and supplies
    B. increase consumption of the most nutritious foods
    C. train subordinates in office techniques
    D. maintain statistical records of retail prices

6.____

7. A budget is BEST described as a(n)   7.____

    A. detailed plan for expenditures
    B. schedule for figuring depreciation of equipment over a period of years
    C. order for necessary equipment
    D. periodic accounting for past expenditures

8. Of the following, the CHIEF reason why a refrigerator door should NOT be left open is   8.____
that the open door will

    A. stop the motor
    B. cause a drop in room temperature
    C. permit the cold air to rise to the top
    D. permit warm air to enter the refrigerator

9. Ovens with thermostatic heat controls should be   9.____

    A. kept closed at all times
    B. opened carefully to prevent jarring
    C. checked periodically for accuracy
    D. disconnected when not in use

10. The term *net weight* means MOST NEARLY the   10.____

    A. actual weight of an item
    B. weight of the container when empty
    C. combined weight of an item and its container
    D. estimated weight of the container alone

11. In requisitioning food, it is LEAST necessary for a dietitian to   11.____

    A. specify the exact quantity desired
    B. secure the signature of the cashier
    C. know the delivery times and order accordingly
    D. know the sizes in which foods are marketed

12. When receiving an order of food, it is INADVISABLE for the dietitian to   12.____

    A. check carefully against the order or requisition
    B. see that all fresh foods are weighed and checked in at the receiving room
    C. check for quality as well as quantity of foods delivered
    D. subtract two pounds tare from the weight of each package delivered in an order

13. Assume that, when inspecting a delivery of vegetables, you find a large amount of sorrel   13.____
mixed in with a bushel of spinach.
The one of the following actions which it is MOST advisable for you to take is to

    A. sort the spinach and sorrel in cleaning and cook them separately to allow greater
       variety in the menu
    B. discard the sorrel as waste
    C. call the purchasing office and arrange to return the spinach as unsatisfactory
    D. place the sorrel in the refrigerator and return it to the driver on his next delivery

14. When purchasing iceberg lettuce, it is ADVISABLE to look for lettuce which is   14.____

    A. loosely headed, with soft curly leaves and a yellow heart
    B. tightly headed, elongated, with coarse green leaves
    C. tightly headed, with medium green outside leaves and a pale green heart
    D. loosely headed, with elongated stalk and rugged curly leaves

15. The term *30-40 prunes* is used to describe the   15.____

    A. number of prunes in a box
    B. particular variety of prunes
    C. brand name of prunes
    D. number of prunes in a pound

16. When ordering chocolate liquor, the dietitian should expect to receive a _____ chocolate.   16.____

    A. solid piece of   B. semi-liquid
    C. liquid   D. glass jar of

17. Of the following, the BEST reason for discarding the green part of potatoes is that it contains a poison known as   17.____

    A. cevitamic acid   B. citric acid
    C. solanine   D. trichinae

18. The number of cans that a standard case of #10 canned apples USUALLY contains is   18.____

    A. 6   B. 12   C. 18   D. 24

19. Of the following, the person MOST closely associated with work in the field of infant behavior and feeding is   19.____

    A. H. Pollack   B. A. Gesell
    C. E.J. Stieglitz   D. J.F. Freeman

20. Of the following, the person BEST known for work in the field of diabetes is   20.____

    A. N. Jolliffe   B. H. Sherman
    C. R.M. Wilder   D. F. Stern

21. An egg which is strictly fresh will   21.____

    A. float in cold water
    B. have a thin and watery egg white
    C. have a swollen egg yolk which is easily broken
    D. sink in cold water

22. Cocoa and chocolate are rich in   22.____

    A. glycogen   B. gum   C. cellulose   D. starch

23. The percentage of protein that is usually converted into glucose in the body is MOST NEARLY   23.____

    A. 49%   B. 58%   C. 67%   D. 78%

24. Of the following vegetables, the one which gives the LARGEST yield, pound for pound, when pureed is   24._____

    A. fresh celery   B. frozen peas
    C. frozen asparagus   D. fresh carrots

25. If the composition of two small rib chops is Protein - 21 grams and Fat - 17 grams, the number of calories in the two chops is MOST NEARLY   25._____

    A. 136   B. 200   C. 237   D. 257

KEY (CORRECT ANSWERS)

1.	D		11.	B
2.	B		12.	D
3.	C		13.	C
4.	B		14.	C
5.	B		15.	D
6.	A		16.	C
7.	A		17.	C
8.	D		18.	A
9.	C		19.	B
10.	A		20.	C

21.	D
22.	D
23.	B
24.	D
25.	C

TEST 2

DIRECTIONS: Each question or incomplete statement is followed by several suggested answers or completions. Select the one that BEST answers the question or completes the statement. *PRINT THE LETTER OF THE CORRECT ANSWER IN THE SPACE AT THE RIGHT.*

1. An APPROPRIATE substitute for sucrose for a patient on a low carbohydrate diet is   1.____

   A. saccharin   B. casec   C. lactose   D. protinol

2. Of the following, the vegetables which are high in protein and, therefore, sometimes substituted for meat are   2.____

   A. green leafy vegetables   B. legumes
   C. root vegetables   D. gourds

3. When planning menus, it is *advisable* to use fish at least once a week because it is a GOOD source of   3.____

   A. iron   B. vitamin C   C. zinc   D. iodine

4. Of the following, the one which is a *non-nutritive* beverage is   4.____

   A. clear tea   B. orangeade
   C. oatmeal gruel   D. cream soda

5. Macaroni is *usually* used as a substitute for   5.____

   A. salad   B. meat   C. potato   D. dessert

6. Bread is dextrinized by   6.____

   A. toasting   B. chopping
   C. drying in open air   D. soaking in hot water

7. Baked custard is used on the menu CHIEFLY   7.____

   A. as a source of vitamin C
   B. because of its high protein content
   C. to add color
   D. as a source of starch

8. The one of the following which is a *non-irritating* food is   8.____

   A. cabbage   B. pickles   C. spaghetti   D. celery

9. Leaves of rhubarb and beets, when boiled in an aluminum container, will clean the container because they contain   9.____

   A. sulphuric acid   B. oxalic acid
   C. ammonia   D. alkali

10. When refinishing a refrigerator ice cube tray, the one of the following which should NOT be used as a coating material is   10.____

   A. aluminum   B. cadmium   C. tin   D. nickel

11. The Department of Health requires the sterilization of eating utensils by 　　11.____

    A. hot air sterilizers   B. ultraviolet rays
    C. chemical solutions   D. water at 180° F

12. Suppose that the dishwashing machine has become clogged with food particles. 　　12.____
Of the following, the action which would be MOST advisable for the dietitian to take
first is to

    A. call the service man to disassemble and clean the machine
    B. instruct the employees assigned to washing dishes about proper scraping of
       dishes
    C. order the employees to prerinse all dishes in order to prevent clogging
    D. remove the strainer tray

13. The one of the following which is the MOST effective way to rid a food storeroom of mice 　　13.____
is to

    A. cement tight all holes which permit invasion
    B. set traps to catch the mice
    C. spread poison around the floor
    D. burn a sulphur candle in the storeroom

14. Black stoves are cleaned BEST by 　　14.____

    A. polishing with an oiled cloth
    B. rubbing with a piece of wax paper
    C. scrubbing with soap and water
    D. heating until they are red hot

15. Of the following, the BEST procedure for cleaning a red quarry tile floor in a hospital 　　15.____
kitchen is to

    A. scrub it, then wax the floor
    B. hose it down with steam
    C. wash it with a strong soap
    D. wash it with a lye

16. After making ice cream, it is MOST important that the machine be 　　16.____

    A. rinsed thoroughly in cold water
    B. sterilized
    C. soaked in soap solution
    D. scrubbed with a brush

17. A dietitian assigned to work with clinic patients should have a basic knowledge of the 　　17.____
foods of foreign-born people.
Of the following, the MOST important reason for this is that

    A. it is interesting and exciting to eat the exotic dishes of foreign lands
    B. such knowledge would prove beyond doubt that poor diet is the cause of poor
       health among the foreign-born

    C.   such knowledge would help the dietitian to plan the patient's prescribed diet around familiar foods

    D.   many foreign dishes are more nutritious than American foods

18.   The clinic dietitian meets several problems of the aging. The one of the following for which she is LEAST responsible is the   18._____

    A.   detection of the onset of chronic degenerative diseases
    B.   conservation of the health of the individual
    C.   re-evaluation of the caloric requirements of aged patients
    D.   overcoming of superstitions and food fallacies

19.   When advising on methods of economizing, the clinic dietitian should instruct patients to AVOID buying   19._____

    A.   foods in quantity, even though storage space permits
    B.   foods that are in season and in abundance on the market
    C.   less expensive cuts of meat
    D.   butter, since there are less expensive substitutes on the market

20.   The one of the following services which is the LEAST basic function of a nutrition clinic is to   20._____

    A.   serve as a teaching center for students
    B.   provide educational programs for patients of all ages
    C.   follow up the nutritional status of individual patients
    D.   secure diet histories of patients for the correction of undesirable food habits

21.   Time and motion studies in the field of dietetics are used PRIMARILY to   21._____

    A.   check on lateness and absence records of employees
    B.   reduce effort and increase efficiency in performing particular tasks
    C.   prepare estimates of time required between requisition and delivery dates
    D.   schedule the daily work assignments for the entire staff

22.   The PRIMARY purpose of using standardized recipes is to   22._____

    A.   aid in controlling food costs
    B.   encourage the cooks to try out new foods
    C.   prepare large quantities of food
    D.   determine the caloric values of foods

23.   The CHIEF advantage of keeping a perpetual inventory of stock items is that   23._____

    A.   supplies may be stored more easily
    B.   there will be less breakage and loss of stock
    C.   it makes it unnecessary to order replacements for stock supplies
    D.   the balance on hand at any time is easily determined

24.   In order to prevent the loss of vitamins in cooking, it is HOST advisable to   24._____

    A.   cover the food completely with water while cooking and boil it rapidly
    B.   peel and soak vegetables in cold water before cooking

C. dice vegetables into small pieces and boil them in an open pot
D. cook vegetables in the shortest possible time in a covered pot containing little water

25. To marinate is to   25._____

A. let foods stand in a specially prepared liquid to add flavor or to tenderize them
B. cook food in liquid just below the boiling point
C. moisten food while cooking by pouring over it drippings or other liquids
D. cook food in water at boiling temperature

KEY (CORRECT ANSWERS)

1.	A		11.	D
2.	B		12.	A
3.	D		13.	A
4.	A		14.	C
5.	C		15.	B
6.	A		16.	B
7.	B		17.	C
8.	C		18.	A
9.	B		19.	D
10.	B		20.	A

21.	B
22.	A
23.	D
24.	D
25.	A

EXAMINATION SECTION
TEST 1

DIRECTIONS: Each question or incomplete statement is followed by several suggested answers or completions. Select the one that BEST answers the question or completes the statement. *PRINT THE LETTER OF THE CORRECT ANSWER IN THE SPACE AT THE RIGHT.*

1. The MOST common cause of death before age 65 is   1.____

    A. cerebrovascular disease   B. malignant neoplasm
    C. heart disease   D. diabetes mellitus
    E. liver cirrhosis

2. Of the following, the disease NOT transmitted by mosquitoes is   2.____

    A. dengue fever
    B. lymphocytic choriomeningitis
    C. western equine encephalitis
    D. St. Louis encephalitis
    E. yellow fever

3. The single MOST effective measure to prevent hookworm infection is   3.____

    A. washing hands
    B. washing clothes daily
    C. cooking food at high temperatures
    D. wearing shoes
    E. none of the above

4. Transmission of tuberculosis in the United States occurs MOST often by   4.____

    A. fomites   B. blood transfusion
    C. inhalation of droplet   D. transplacentally
    E. milk

5. The second MOST common cause of death in the United States is   5.____

    A. accident   B. cancer
    C. cerebrovascular disease   D. heart disease
    E. AIDS

6. All of the following bacteria are spread through fecal-oral transmission EXCEPT   6.____

    A. haemophilus influenza type B   B. campylobacter
    C. escherichia coli   D. salmonella
    E. shigella

7. Routine immunization is particularly important for children in day care because pre-school-aged children currently have the highest age specific incidence of all of the following EXCEPT   7.____

    A. H-influenzae type B   B. neisseria meningitis
    C. measles   D. rubella
    E. pertussis

8. Hand washing and masks are necessary for physical contact with all of the following patients EXCEPT   8.____

   A. lassa fever
   B. diphtheria
   C. coxsackie virus disease
   D. varicella
   E. plaque

9. Control measures for prevention of tick-borne infections include all of the following EXCEPT: 9.____

   A. Tick-infested area should be avoided whenever possible.
   B. If a tick-infested area is entered, protective clothing that covers the arms, legs, and other exposed area should be worn.
   C. Tick/insect repellent should be applied to the skin.
   D. Ticks should be removed promptly.
   E. Daily inspection of pets and removal of ticks is not indicated.

10. The PRINCIPAL reservoir of giardia lamblia infection is   10.____

    A. humans
    B. mosquitoes
    C. rodents
    D. sandflies
    E. cats

11. Most community-wide epidemics of giardia lamblia infection result from   11.____

    A. inhalation of droplets
    B. eating infected meats
    C. eating contaminated eggs
    D. drinking contaminated water
    E. blood transfusions

12. Epidemics of giardia lamblia occurring in day care centers are USUALLY caused by   12.____

    A. inhalation of droplets
    B. person-to-person contact
    C. fecal and oral contact
    D. eating contaminated food
    E. all of the above

13. Measures of the proportion of the population exhibiting a phenomenon at a particular time is called the   13.____

    A. incidence
    B. prevalence
    C. prospective study
    D. cohort study
    E. all of the above

14. The occurrence of an event or characteristic over a period of time is called   14.____

    A. incidence
    B. prevalence
    C. specificity
    D. case control study
    E. cohort study

15. All of the following are live attenuated viral vaccines EXCEPT   15.____

    A. measles
    B. mumps
    C. rubella
    D. rabies
    E. yellow fever

128

16. Chlorinating air-cooling towers can prevent   16.____

   A. scarlet fever   B. impetigo
   C. typhoid fever   D. mycobacterium tuberculosis
   E. legionnaire's disease

17. Eliminating the disease causing agent may be done by all of the following methods   17.____
    EXCEPT

   A. chemotherapeutic   B. cooling
   C. heating   D. chlorinating
   E. disinfecting

18. Which of the following medications is used to eliminate pharyngeal carriage of neisseria   18.____
    meningitidis?

   A. Penicillin   B. Rifampin
   C. Isoniazid   D. Erythromycin
   E. Gentamicin

19. Post-exposure prophylaxis is recommended for rabies after the bite of all of the following   19.____
    animals EXCEPT

   A. chipmunks   B. skunks   C. raccoons
   D. bats   E. foxes

20. To destroy the spores of clostridium botulinum, canning requires a temperature of AT   20.____
    LEAST _____°C.

   A. 40   B. 60   C. 80   D. 100   E. 120

21. All of the following are killed or fractionated vaccines EXCEPT   21.____

   A. hepatitis B   B. yellow fever
   C. H-influenza type B   D. pneumococcus
   E. rabies

22. Of the following, the disease NOT spready by food is   22.____

   A. typhoid fever   B. shigellosis
   C. typhus   D. cholera
   E. legionellosis

23. In the United States, the HIGHEST attack rate of sheigella infection occurs in children   23.____
    between _____ of age.

   A. 1 to 6 months   B. 6 months to 1 year
   C. 1 to 4 years   D. 6 to 10 years
   E. 10 to 15 years

24. Risk factors for cholera include all of the following EXCEPT   24.____

   A. occupational exposure
   B. lower socioeconomic
   C. unsanitary condition
   D. high socioeconomic
   E. high population density in low income areas

25. The MOST common cause of traveler's diarrhea is   25.____

    A. escherichia coli   B. shigella
    C. salmonella   D. cholera
    E. campalobacter

_____

KEY (CORRECT ANSWERS)

1.	C		11.	D
2.	B		12.	B
3.	D		13.	B
4.	C		14.	A
5.	B		15.	D
6.	A		16.	E
7.	B		17.	B
8.	C		18.	B
9.	E		19.	A
10.	A		20.	E

21.	B
22.	C
23.	C
24.	D
25.	A

_____

TEST 2

DIRECTIONS: Each question or incomplete statement is followed by several suggested answers or completions. Select the one that BEST answers the question or completes the statement. *PRINT THE LETTER OF THE CORRECT ANSWER IN THE SPACE AT THE RIGHT.*

1. The increased prevalence of entamoeba histolytica infection results from   1.____

    A. lower socioeconomic status in endemic area
    B. institutionalized (especially mentally retarded) population
    C. immigrants from endemic area
    D. promiscuous homosexual men
    E. all of the above

2. The MOST common infection acquired in the hospital is _____ infection.   2.____

    A. surgical wound   B. lower respiratory tract
    C. urinary tract   D. bloodstream
    E. gastrointestinal

3. The etiologic agent of Rocky Mountain spotted fever is   3.____

    A. rickettsia prowazekii   B. rickettsia rickettsii
    C. rickettsia akari   D. coxiella burnetii
    E. rochalimaena quintana

4. The annual death rate for injuries per 100,000 in both sexes is HIGHEST in those   4.____
    _____ years of age.

    A. 1 to 10   B. 10 to 20   C. 30 to 40
    D. 50 to 60   E. 80 to 90

5. The death rate per 100,000 population due to motor vehicle accident is HIGHEST among   5.____

    A. whites   B. blacks
    C. Asians   D. native Americans
    E. Spanish surnamed

6. Among the following, the HIGHEST rate of homicide occurs in   6.____

    A. whites   B. blacks
    C. native Americans   D. Asians
    E. Spanish surnamed

7. All of the following are true statements regarding coronary heart disease EXCEPT: 7.____

    A. About 4.6 million Americans have coronary heart disease.
    B. Men have a greater risk of MI and sudden death.
    C. Women have a greater risk of angina pectoris.
    D. 25% of coronary heart disease death occurs in individuals under the age of 65 years.
    E. White women have a greater risk of MI and sudden death.

8. Major risk factors for coronary heart disease include all of the following EXCEPT   8.____

    A. smoking
    B. elevated blood pressure
    C. obesity
    D. high level of serum cholesterol
    E. family history of coronary heart disease

9. The MOST common cancer in American men is   9.____

    A. stomach   B. lung   C. leukemia
    D. prostate   E. skin

10. The HIGHEST incidence of prostate cancer occurs in _____ Americans.   10.____

    A. white   B. black   C. Chinese
    D. Asian   E. Spanish

11. All of the following are risk factors for cervical cancer EXCEPT   11.____

    A. smoking
    B. low socioeconomic condition
    C. first coital experience after age 20
    D. multiple sexual partners
    E. contracting a sexually transmitted disease

12. All of the following are independent adverse prognostic factors for lung cancer EXCEPT   12.____

    A. female sex
    B. short duration of symptom
    C. small cell histology
    D. metastatic disease at time of diagnosis
    E. persistently elevated CEA

13. Assuming vaccines with 80% efficacy were available in limited quantity, which vaccine among the following should be given to a military recruit?   13.____

    A. Polio   B. Pseudomonas
    C. Meningococcus   D. Influenza
    E. None of the above

14. Among the following, the vaccine which should be administered to children with sickle cell disease is   14.____

    A. influenza   B. meningococcus
    C. pseudomonas   D. pneumococcal
    E. yellow fever

15. All of the following are correct statements concerning gastric carcinoma in the United States EXCEPT: 15.____

    A. The risk for males is 2.2 times greater than for females.
    B. The incidence is increased.
    C. The risk is higher in persons with pernicious anemia than for the general population.

D. City dwellers have an increased risk of stomach cancer.

E. Workers with high levels of exposure to nickle and rubber are at increased risk.

16. During the first year of life, a condition that can be detected by screening is   16.____

    A. hypothyroidism
    B. RH incompatibility
    C. phenylketonuria
    D. congenital dislocation of the hip
    E. all of the above

17. The major reservoir of the spread of tuberculosis within a hospital is through   17.____

    A. patients   B. custodial staff
    C. doctors   D. nursing staff
    E. undiagnosed cases

18. All of the following statements are true regarding tuberculosis EXCEPT: 18.____

    A. Droplet nuclei are the major vehicle for the spread of tuberculosis infection.
    B. The highest incidence is among white Americans.
    C. There is a higher incidence of tuberculosis in prison than in the general population.
    D. HIV infection is a significant independent risk factor for the development of tuberculosis.
    E. A single tubercle bacillus, once having gained access to the terminal air spaces, could establish infection.

19. The human papiloma virus is associated with   19.____

    A. kaposi sarcoma
    B. hepatoma
    C. cervical neoplasia
    D. nasopharyngeal carcinoma
    E. none of the above

20. General recommendations for prevention of sexually transmitted diseases include all of the following EXCEPT   20.____

    A. contact tracing   B. disease reporting
    C. barrier methods   D. prophylactic antibiotic use
    E. patient education

21. Syphilis remains an important sexually transmitted disease because of all of the following EXCEPT its   21.____

    A. public health heritage
    B. effect on perinatal morbidity and mortality
    C. association with HIV transmission
    D. escalating rate among black teenagers
    E. inability to be prevented

22. Which of the following statements about homicide is NOT true? Approximately

    22.____

    A. forty percent are committed by friends and acquaintances
    B. twenty percent is committed by spouse
    C. fifteen percent is committed by a member of the victim's family
    D. fifteen percent is committed by strangers
    E. fifteen percent are labeled *relationship unknown*

23. Conditions for which screening has proven cost-effective include

    23.____

    A. phenylketonuria   B. iron deficiency anemia
    C. lead poisoning   D. tuberculosis
    E. all of the above

24. Suicide is MOST common among

    24.____

    A. whites   B. blacks
    C. hispanics   D. Asians
    E. none of the above

25. The MOST frequenty used method of suicide is

    25.____

    A. hanging   B. poisoning by gases
    C. firearms   D. drug overdose
    E. drowning

KEY (CORRECT ANSWERS)

1.	E		11.	C
2.	C		12.	A
3.	B		13.	C
4.	E		14.	D
5.	D		15.	B
6.	B		16.	E
7.	E		17.	E
8.	C		18.	B
9.	D		19.	C
10.	B		20.	D

21.	E
22.	B
23.	E
24.	A
25.	C

EXAMINATION SECTION
TEST 1

DIRECTIONS: Each question or incomplete statement is followed by several suggested
answers or completions. Select the one that BEST answers the question or
completes the statement. *PRINT THE LETTER OF THE CORRECT ANSWER
IN THE SPACE AT THE RIGHT.*

1. _____ accounts for the LARGEST percentage of personal health care expenditures in the   1._____
United States.
    A. Physician services   B. Hospital care
    C. Nursing homes   D. Drug and medical supplies
    E. Dentist services

2. MOST health care expenses in the United States are paid by   2._____
    A government programs   B. Medicare
    B. Medicaid   D. private health insurance
    E. out-of-pocket payments

3. A physician is NOT legally required to report   3._____
    A. births and deaths
    B. suspected child abuse
    C. gunshot wounds
    D. a child with croup
    E. a child with shigella dysentery

4. Diseases more likely to occur in blacks than whites include all of the following EXCEPT   4._____
    A. thalassemia   B. sickle cell disease
    C. sarcoidosis   D. tuberculosis
    E. hypertension

5. Among the United States population, what malignant tumor has the greatest incidence?   5._____
    A. Breast   B. Prostate
    C. Lung   D. Colon
    E. Stomach

6. The MOST frequent cause of chronic obstructive pulmonary disease is   6._____

    A. frequent upper respiratory infection
    B. smoking
    C. family member with asthma
    D. drug abuse
    E. infantile paralysis

7. The ultimate legal responsibility for quality of medical care provided in the hospital rests   7._____
upon the
    A. hospital administrator
    B. chief of nursing staff
    C. director of the hospital
    D. principal nurse
    E. patient's physician

8. Routine screening for diabetes is recommended for all patients EXCEPT those with   8._____
    A. family history of diabetes
    B. glucose abnormalities associated with pregnancy
    C. marked obesity
    D. an episode of hypoglycemia as a newborn
    E. physical abnormality, such as circulatory dysfunction and frank vascular
       impairment

9. Low maternal AFP level is associated with   9._____
    A. spina bifida   B. Down syndrome
    C. meningocele   D. hypothyroidism
    E. Niemann Pick disease

10. All of the following are skin disorders EXCEPT   10._____
    A. psoriasis   B. eczema
    C. scleroderma   D. gout
    E. shingles

11. All of the following are true statements regarding osteoporosis EXCEPT:
                                                                                              11._____
    A. The reduction of bone mass in osteoporosis causes the bone to be susceptible
       to fracture.
    B. Bone loss occurs with advancing age in both men and women.
    C. In developing countries, high parity has been associated with decreased bone
       mass and increased risk of fracture.
    D. Thin women are at higher risk than obese women.
    E. Daughters of women with osteoporosis tend to have lower bone mass than other
       women of their age.

12. The MOST common type of occupational disease is   12._____
    A. hearing loss   B. dermatitis
    B. pneumoconiosis   D. pulmonary fibrosis
    E. none of the above

13. The incidence of Down syndrome in the United States is about 1 in _____ births.   13._____

    A. 700   B. 1200   C. 1500   D. 2000   E. 10000

14. Lyme disease and Rocky Mountain spotted fever CANNOT be prevented by   14._____
    A. door and window screen use
    B. hand washing
    C. wearing protective clothing
    D. using insect repellent
    E. immediate tick removal

15. Individuals with egg allergies can be safely administered all of the following vaccines   15._____
    EXCEPT
    A. MMR (Measles-Mumps-Rubella)
    B. hepatitis B
    C. influenza
    D. DTaP (Diphtheria-Tetanus-Whooping Cough)
    E. none of the above

16. Lifetime prevalence of cocaine use is HIGHER among   16._____
    A. Hispanics   B. blacks   C. whites   D. Asians
    E. none of the above

17. The effectiveness of preventive measures against chronic illness is BEST determined   17._____
from trends in
    A. incidence   B. mortality   C. prevalence   D. frequency of complication
    E. all of the above

18. Primary prevention of congenital heart disease includes all of the following established   18._____
measures EXCEPT:
    A. Genetic counseling of potential parents and families with congenital heart disease
    B. Avoidance of exposure to viral diseases during pregnancy
    C. Avoidance of all vaccines to all children which eliminate the reservoir of infection
    D. Avoidance of radiation during pregnancy
    E. Avoidance of exposure during first trimester of pregnancy to gas fumes, air pollution, cigarettes, alcohol

19. All of the following are true statements regarding genetic factors associated with   19._____
congenital heart disease EXCEPT:
    A. The offspring of a parent with a congenital heart disease has a malformation rate ranging from 1.4% to 16.1%.
    B. Identical twins are both affected 25 to 30% of the time.
    C. Single gene disorder accounts for less than 1% of all cardiac congenital anomalies.
    D. Environment does not play a role in cardiac anomalies
    E. Other finding of familial aggregation suggests polygenic factors.

20. MOST likely inadequately supplied in strict vegetarian adults is   20._____
    A. vitamin A   B. thiamin   C. vitamin B_{12} D. niacin   E. protein

21. The MOST common reservoir of acquired immune deficiency syndrome is   21._____

    A. humans   B. mosquitoes   C. cats   D. dogs   E. monkeys

22. A definitive indicator of active tuberculosis is   22._____
    A. chronic persistent cough
    B. positive PPD
    C. night sweats
    D. positive sputum test
    E. hilar adenopathy on chest x-ray

23. Which of the following is NOT a risk factor for development of colorectal carcinoma?   23._____
    A. Familial polyposis coli   B. Furcot's syndrome
    C. High fiber diet   D. Increased dietary fat
    E. Villous polyps

24. According to the American Cancer Society, starting at the age of 50, men and women at   24._____
average risk for developing colorectal cancer should follow which of the following
screening regimens?
    A. Colonoscopy every ten years
    B. Flexible sigmoidoscopy every two years
    C. Double-contrast barium enema every two years
    D. CT colonography (virtual colonoscopy) every year
    E. None of the above

25. The MOST common malignancy among women is of the   25._____
    A. lung   B. breast   C. ovary   D. rectum   E. vagina

KEY (CORRECT ANSWERS)

1.	B		11.	C
2.	D		12.	A
3.	D		13.	A
4.	A		14.	B
5.	D		15.	C
6.	B		16.	C
7.	E		17.	C
8.	D		18.	C
9.	B		19.	D
10.	D		20.	C

21.	A
22.	D
23.	C
24.	A
25.	B

TEST 2

DIRECTIONS: Each question or incomplete statement is followed by several suggested answers or completions. Select the one that BEST answers the question or completes the statement. *PRINT THE LETTER OF THE CORRECT ANSWER IN THE SPACE AT THE RIGHT.*

1. The MOST common cause of death due to malignancy among females in the United States is from   1._____

    A. lung cancer   B. ovarian cancer
    C. skin cancer   D. colon and rectum cancer
    B. leukemia

2. Medicare provides health coverage to people   2._____
    A. under 20 years of age
    B. who work of all ages
    C. greater than 65 years of age and end-stage renal dialysis patients
    D. under five years of age who require long-term hospitalization
    E. who need out-patient care only

3. Insurance approaches to contain cost include managed care plans. A popular managed care approach has been   3._____
    A. Medicare
    B. Medicaid
    C. HMO's
    D. institutional reimbursement
    E. none of the above

4. The occupational exposure that may lead to chronic interstitial pulmonary disease is   4._____
    A. silicosis   B. pneumoconiosis
    C. asbestosis   D. farmer's lung
    E. all of the above

5. The principal mode of transmission of hepatitis A virus is   5._____
    A. blood transfusion   B. droplet nuclei
    C. fecal and oral route   D. mosquitoes
    E. deer flies

6. The leading cause of death among diabetics after 20 years of diabetes is by   6._____
    A. infection
    B. cerebrovascular accident
    C. renal and cardiovascular disease
    D. diabetic ketoacidosis
    E. malignancy

7. A breast-fed infant may require a supplementation of vitamin   7._____
    A. E   B. B_{12} C. K   D. D   E. A

8. The MOST common organism associated with chronic active gastritis is   8._____
    A. salmonella   B. shigella
    C. campylobacter pylori   D. staphylococcus
    E. rota virus

9. The large proportion of tuberculosis in older persons is due to   9._____
   A. recent exposure to tuberculosis
   B. reactivation of latent infection
   C. malnutrition
   D. immunosuppression
   E. substance abuse

10. The leading vector-borne disease in the United States is   10._____
    A. lyme disease
    B. Rocky Mountain spotted fever
    C. ehrlichiosis
    D. Q fever
    E. yellow fever

11. The malarial species causing the MOST fatal illness is   11._____
    A. P. vivax   B. P. falciparum
    C. P. malariae   D. P. cuale
    E. none of the above

Questions 12-16.

DIRECTIONS: Match the disease in Questions 12 through 16 with the associated animal in
            Column I.

12. Brucellosis   COLUMN I   12._____

13. Psittacosis   A. Bird   13._____
                                   B. Swine
14. Rabies   C. Rabbit   14._____
                                   D. Skunk
15. Tularemia   E. Cats   15._____

16. Toxoplasmosis   16._____

Questions 17-22.

DIRECTIONS: Match the trade in Questions 17 through 22 with the related occupational cancer in Column I.

17. Pipefitters

18. Rubber industry workers

19. Radiologist

20. Woodworkers

21. Textile workers

22. Chemists

COLUMN I

A. Carcinoma of the bladder
B. Mesothelioma
C. Hodgkin's disease
D. Leukemia
E. Brain cancer
F. Carcinoma of nasal cavity

17._____

18._____

19._____

20._____

21._____

22._____

Questions 23-25.

DIRECTIONS: Match the biostatistical description in Questions 23 through 25 with the related term in Column I.

23. The presence of an event or characteristic at a single point in time

24. Require a long period of observation

25. The occurrence of an event or characteristic over a period of time

COLUMN I

A. Incidence
B. Prevalence
C. Cohort study

23._____

24._____

25._____

KEY (CORRECT ANSWERS)

1. A		11. B	
2. C		12. B	
3. C		13. A	
4. E		14. D	
5. C		15. C	
6. C		16. E	
7. D		17. B	
8. C		18. A	
9. B		19. D	
10. A		20. C	

21.	F
22.	E
23.	B
24.	C
25.	A

EXAMINATION SECTION
TEST 1

DIRECTIONS: Each question or incomplete statement is followed by several suggested answers or completions. Select the one that BEST answers the question or completes the statement. *PRINT THE LETTER OF THE CORRECT ANSWER IN THE SPACE AT THE RIGHT.*

1. In regard to first aid procedures, priority in treatment should be given FIRST to cases of   1.____

   A. internal poisoning
   B. severe eye injuries
   C. stoppage of breathing
   D. severe bleeding at the neck

2. The American Red Cross advocates that for an insect sting on the neck, the first aider   2.____
   apply to the injured part

   A. a cut in the skin at the spot to encourage bleeding in order to remove impurities
   B. suction in order to remove the injected toxin
   C. ice applications
   D. hot, wet applications

3. The group of symptoms BEST describing a case of shock is   3.____

   A. extreme thirst, skin dry, breathing deep, pulse irregular
   B. face flushed, pulse full, pupils constricted, nauseous-ness
   C. pulse absent, skin hot, breathing heavy, face ashen
   D. body weakness, skin moist, pupils dilated, breathing shallow

4. According to the American Red Cross, the four types of wounds are   4.____

   A. scrapes, cuts, burns, stabs
   B. punctures, lacerations, incisions, abrasions
   C. friction burns, open blisters, gashes, punctures
   D. scratches, infections, sores, bleeding cuts

5. When administering first aid to a pupil experiencing an epileptic attack, the teacher   5.____
   should FIRST

   A. loosen clothing about the neck and chest
   B. remove the victim to a room other than a classroom filled with pupils
   C. place an object between the victim's upper and lower teeth on one side of the
      mouth
   D. apply an ammonia ampule to the victim's nostrils

6. In the execution of the back pressure-arm lift method of artificial respiration, all of the   6.____
   following are correct procedures EXCEPT the one in which the operator

   A. places the victims in the prone position with the face turned to one side
   B. rocks foward with bent elbows as he exerts pressure at a 70° angle
   C. draws the arms of the victim upward and toward him during the final step of the
      cycle
   D. repeats the cycle at a steady rate of 12 times per minute

7. In second or third degree burns, all of the following are correct first aid procedures EXCEPT

    A. applying mineral oil to the area
    B. giving fluids by mouth
    C. providing immediate first aid for shock
    D. covering the burned area with sterile dressing

7.____

8. Of the following symptoms a person might display after receiving a blow to the head, the one MOST indicative of serious injury is

    A. pallor
    B. swelling
    C. dizziness
    D. inequality in size of pupils of the eye

8.____

9. When reassuring a victim of an accident, of the following, it is MOST advisable to

    A. explain his condition to him as you find it and state you will stay with him
    B. tell him what first aid steps you are going to take and how they will help him
    C. state to the victim that, since there is no doctor around, you will take his place
    D. keep the victim talking about the accident to relieve tension

9.____

10. The rate at which artificial respiration should be given to adults is

    A. about 12 times a minute
    B. about 20 times a minute
    C. as fast as you can work
    D. slightly faster than normal breathing

10.____

KEY (CORRECT ANSWERS)

1.	D	6.	B
2.	C	7.	A
3.	D	8.	D
4.	B	9.	B
5.	C	10.	A

TEST 2

DIRECTIONS: Each question or incomplete statement is followed by several suggested answers or completions. Select the one that BEST answers the question or completes the statement. *PRINT THE LETTER OF THE CORRECT ANSWER IN THE SPACE AT THE RIGHT.*

1. In rendering the mouth-to-mouth method of artificial respiration, the one hand of the operator should

    1.____

    A. cover the victim's nose and the other hand should be placed on the chest
    B. be on the ground near the victim's shoulder and in such position as to assist the other hand in maintaining equal support of his body weight
    C. hold the victim's jaw up and back and the other hand should pinch the victim's nostrils together
    D. be placed around the victim's mouth and the other hand should hold the nape of the victim's neck rigid

2. In the case of a severely burned victim who needs fluids, of the following, it is MOST advisable to give him at fifteen-minute intervals

    2.____

    A. a full cup of hot tea or hot coffee
    B. a teaspoonful of spirits of ammonia in a glass of water
    C. half-glass doses of one-half teaspoon of table salt and of baking soda in a quart of water
    D. a mild stimulant

3. In caring for burns, the first aider should

    3.____

    A. break the blisters caused by the burn
    B. apply wet dressings to the burned area
    C. apply large amounts of lukewarm water to a chemical burn before treating the burn
    D. remove scorched clothing on or near the burn

4. A person, in rendering first aid, should

    4.____

    A. administer medication internally
    B. apply antiseptics to broken skin
    C. attempt to remove foreign bodies from eyes
    D. use the method of artificial respiration best known to him

5. In cases of shock, the first aider should elevate the lower part of the victim's body is

    5.____

    A. the blood loss is great
    B. he complains of pain at a fracture site in the lower extremity
    C. there is a head injury
    D. breathing is difficult

6. When rendering first aid to a diabetic who suddenly becomes confused, incoherent, and faint, the FIRST thing to be done is to

    6.____

    A. keep him warm and comfortable until a doctor arrives
    B. give him some form of sugar if he can swallow
    C. use a mild stimulant to keep him from losing consciousness
    D. take steps to summon an ambulance

7. During the winter months, in cases of first aid care for victims of shock, the first aider should   7.___

    A. wrap the victim in excess covering while waiting for the arrival of the doctor
    B. cover the victim sparingly in spite of a possible low temperature
    C. always apply hot water bottles to the victim's body
    D. protect the victim's body so that a flushed condition of the skin appears and is then maintained

8. In order to minimize the possibility of infection, the first aider, when caring for a wound, should   8.___

    A. wash the body surface toward the wound before applying a gauze dressing
    B. use soap and clean running tap water on both the wound and its surrounding area
    C. apply a two percent iodine solution as his first step in treating the wound
    D. cover the wound with adhesive tape in order to prevent contact with germs

9. If a particle is on the eyeball, one should NOT   9.___

    A. close his eyes for a few minutes in order to allow the tears to wash out the foreign matter
    B. grasp the lashes of the upper lid and draw it out and down over the lower lid in order to dislodge the particle
    C. use an eye dropper in order to flush the eye so that the particle will float out of the eye
    D. examine the eye in order to determine the location of the foreign particle and, when found, remove it from the eyeball by touching lightly with the moistened corner of a clean handkerchief

10. Of the following concerning mouth-to-mouth resuscitation, the operator can BEST be sure that no obstruction exists in the victim's air passage by following his first blowing efforts with a   10.___

    A. sharp tilt backward of the victim's head so that the chin points almost directly upward
    B. forceful opening of the victim's mouth as the victim's nostrils are held in a closed position
    C. removal of his mouth by turning his head to the side in order to listen for the return rush of air from the victim's body
    D. removal of mucous and foreign matter in the victim's mouth

---

KEY (CORRECT ANSWERS)

1.	C	6.	B
2.	C	7.	B
3.	B	8.	B
4.	D	9.	D
5.	A	10.	C

TEST 3

DIRECTIONS: Each question or incomplete statement is followed by several suggested answers or completions. Select the one that BEST answers the question or completes the statement. *PRINT THE LETTER OF THE CORRECT ANSWER IN THE SPACE AT THE RIGHT.*

1. The universal antidote to be administered in poisoning cases if no specific antidote is known consists of   1.____

    A. several teaspoonfuls of baking soda in half a glass of water
    B. a large glass of milk diluted with an equal amount of water
    C. one part tea, two parts crumbled burnt toast, one part milk of magnesia
    D. one part milk, one part egg white, one part water

2. In the case of severe bleeding from a hand, the first aider should IMMEDIATELY   2.____

    A. locate the pressure point above the wound and apply digital pressure at that point
    B. apply pressure directly on the wound with clean gauze or a towel
    C. apply a tourniquet in order to limit the flow of blood from the artery to the wound
    D. locate the pressure point and apply a tourniquet at that point

3. The INCORRECT association of first aid bandage and body area of use is   3.____

    A. four-tailed bandage - nose
    B. cravat bandage - knee
    C. triangular bandage - head
    D. figure-eight bandage - chest

4. With victims of shock, when medical help is not immediate, water should NOT be given to those who have   4.____

    A. suffered marked bleeding
    B. burns involving more than ten percent of the body surface
    C. a penetrating abdominal wound
    D. a fracture of the femur

5. The MAIN objective in first aid care for a victim of poison by mouth is to   5.____

    A. first induce vomiting
    B. dilute the poison
    C. give an antidote
    D. look around for tell-tale evidence of the poison

6. The LATEST accepted method (American Red Cross) of administering artificial respiration is known as the _____ method.   6.____

    A. back-pressure arm-lift   B. chest-pressure arm-lift
    C. mouth-to-mouth   D. prone pressure

7. All of the following statements regarding first aid care are correct EXCEPT: 7.____

    A. Soap and clean water may be used to wash the wounded area in case of minor wounds

    B. A modified back-pressure arm-lift method of artificial respiration is recommended for infants and children under 4 years of age

    C. Direct pressure is recommended for most cases of severe bleeding

    D. Shock victims should be kept slightly cool rather than *toasting* warm with little or no surface covering used on warm days

8. In poisoning, the first aider should induce vomiting for all of the following taken through the mouth EXCEPT 8.____

    A. lye   B. barbiturates

    C. mushrooms   D. iodine

9. A recommended first aid procedure in the treatment of heat stroke is to 9.____

    A. give a stimulant

    B. keep the head lower than the chest

    C. apply external heat to the body

    D. sponge the body with lukewarm water

10. Of the following, the distinctive symptom in cases of heat stroke is 10.____

    A. a desire to sleep   B. nausea

    C. absence of perspiration   D. dizziness

KEY (CORRECT ANSWERS)

1.	C	6.	C
2.	B	7.	B
3.	D	8.	A
4.	C	9.	D
5.	B	10.	C

TEST 4

DIRECTIONS: Each question or incomplete statement is followed by several suggested answers or completions. Select the one that BEST answers the question or completes the statement. *PRINT THE LETTER OF THE CORRECT ANSWER IN THE SPACE AT THE RIGHT.*

1. All of the following are recommended first aid measures for insect bites and stings EXCEPT the application of   1.____

    A. a compress moistened with ammonia water
    B. calamine lotion
    C. ice
    D. light massage in order to remove the sting

2. According to the American Red Cross, the INCORRECT association of type of bandage and injury is   2.____

    A. four-tail bandage - fracture of the jaw
    B. spiral-reverse bandage - wound on the forearm
    C. figure-of-eight bandage - sprained ankle
    D. cravat bandage - eye injury

3. A compound fracture is one in which the bone is   3.____

    A. broken in many pieces
    B. broken with a connecting wound on the surface of the body
    C. twisted apart
    D. broken longitudinally

4. One of the shop workers strikes heavily against the wall. You recognize that he is in a state of shock because of his   4.____

    A. strong pulse
    B. regular but deep breathing
    C. moist, pale skin
    D. high body temperature

5. According to the American Red Cross, first aid care for an individual who gives evidence of possible insulin reaction when there is no other reason to account for the trouble includes the   5.____

    A. usual treatment for shock
    B. giving of candy or sugar to the victim
    C. application of artificial respiration
    D. swallowing of a stimulant

6. In caring for frostbite cases, one should   6.____

    A. apply woolen material to the injured area
    B. rub the injured part with snow
    C. massage the affected part
    D. have the victim soak the injured part in water as hot as possible

7. When applying wet applications to infected wounds, one should AVOID   7.____

    A. boiling the water prior to its use
    B. adding salt to the liquid
    C. half-hour periods of application followed by alternate free periods of the same
        length
    D. having the solution hot

8. According to the American Red Cross, tourniquets may be applied in all of the following   8.____
    situations EXCEPT

    A. when severe bleeding involves an extremity in which large arteries are severed
    B. to individuals who are known to be allergic to a bee or wasp sting, if the sting is on
        an extremity
    C. in cases where there is partial severance of a body part accompanied by severe
        bleeding
    D. to a limb in which there is an infected wound and there is indication of a spread of
        the infection

9. According to the American Red Cross, it is MOST NEARLY accurate to state that the   9.____
    danger of tetanus is present in _____ wounds.

    A. puncture   B. lacerated
    C. incised   D. all

10. All of the following men have developed a method of artificial respiration EXCEPT   10.____

    A. Schafer   B. Neilsen
    C. Cureton   D. Silvester

_____

KEY (CORRECT ANSWERS)

1.	D	6.	A
2.	A	7.	D
3.	B	8.	D
4.	C	9.	D
5.	B	10.	C

_____

TEST 5

DIRECTIONS: Each question or incomplete statement is followed by several suggested answers or completions. Select the one that BEST answers the question or completes the statement. *PRINT THE LETTER OF THE CORRECT ANSWER IN THE SPACE AT THE RIGHT.*

1. The recommended American Red Cross first aid care for sunburns in which the skin is blistered is the application of

    A. a burn ointment or medicated cream
    B. butter or oleomargarine
    C. a sterile, dry dressing
    D. a dressing saturated with a warm salt solution

1.____

2. The MOST serious harm from tiny foreign objects on the eye surface is

    A. their irritating effect
    B. the danger of their becoming embedded in the outer layer of the eyeball
    C. their creating an increased secretion of tears
    D. their interference with the individual's normal vision

2.____

3. All of the following are complete fractures EXCEPT a(n) _____ fracture.

    A. impacted   B. Greenstick
    C. Colles'   D. Pott's

3.____

4. The CORRECT statement in regard to the first aid care for burns is:

    A. Burns must be treated only with moist materials
    B. Greasy substances are the best medicines for all types of burns
    C. Burns must be treated only with dry materials
    D. The depth to which the body tissues are injured determines the first aid care

4.____

5. In applying a strapping to a sprained ankle, the person applying the strapping should

    A. pull the tape tight over the bony prominence of the ankle
    B. bind the toes as well as the rest of the foot
    C. have the injured foot in a position of 90 dorsi-flexion
    D. have the injured person keep the knee of the injured leg straight

5.____

6. To clean a thermometer after use, the American Red Cross advises the use of

    A. formaldehyde   B. cool water and soap
    C. peroxide   D. liquid soap in hot water

6.____

7. Hot applications should be applied

    A. in case of a sting from an insect
    B. in case of nosebleed
    C. to an ankle immediately after it is sprained
    D. none of the above cases

7.____

8. If a victim complains of increased pain after traction has been applied to a fractured leg, the first aider would MOST likely conclude that

    A. the traction bands are too loose
    B. the traction bands are too tight
    C. a tourniquet must be applied
    D. the simple fracture has turned into a compound fracture

8.____

9. Care of an unconscious victim, when the cause of unconsciousness is unknown, is based upon the

    A. pulse rate   B. odor of the breath
    C. color of the face   D. location of the accident

9.____

10. A victim of heat exhaustion will MOST likely have

    A. a moist skin   B. a strong pulse
    C. a red face   D. high temperature

10.____

KEY (CORRECT ANSWERS)

1.	C	6.	B
2.	B	7.	D
3.	B	8.	A
4.	D	9.	C
5.	C	10.	A

FIRST AID

Table of Contents

FIRST AID

Basic Principles and Practices

CAUTION
These are emergency actions only. Always call a doctor if possible. If you cannot get a doctor or trained first-aider and the injured person is in danger of losing his life, take one of the six emergency actions described in this section.

BUT, FIRST, OBSERVE THESE GENERAL RULES:
Keep the injured person lying down, with his head level with the rest of his body unless he has a head injury. In that case raise his head slightly. Cover him and keep him warm.

Don't move the injured person to determine whether emergency action is necessary. If he is NOT in danger of bleeding to death, or is NOT suffocating or has NOT been severely burned, or is NOT in shock, IT IS BETTER FOR THE UNTRAINED PERSON TO LEAVE HIM ALONE.
Do NOT give an unconscious or semiconscious person anything to drink.
Do NOT let an injured person see his wounds.
Reassure him and keep him comfortable.

EMERGENCY ACTIONS
   I.   FOR BLEEDING
          TAKE THIS EMERGENCY ACTION
              Apply pressure directly over the wound. Use a first aid dressing, clean cloth, or even the bare hand. When bleeding has been controlled, add extra layers of cloth and bandage firmly. Do NOT remove the dressing. If the wound is in an arm or leg, elevate it with pillows or substitutes. Do NOT use a tourniquet except as a last resort.

   II. FOR BURNS
          TAKE THIS EMERGENCY ACTION
              Remove clothing covering the burn unless it sticks. Cover the burned area with a clean dry dressing or several layers of cloth folded into a pad. Apply a bandage over the pad, tightly enough to keep out the air. Don't remove the pad. DON'T USE GREASE, OIL OR ANY OINTMENT EXCEPT ON A DOCTOR'S ORDER. On chemical burns, such as caused by acid or lye, wash the burn thoroughly with water before covering with a dry dressing.

   III. FOR BROKEN BONES
          TAKE THIS EMERGENCY ACTION
              Unless it is absolutely necessary to move a person with a broken bone, don't do anything except apply an ice bag to the injured area to relieve pain. If you must move him, splint the broken bone first so the broken bone ends cannot move. Use a board, thick bundle of newspapers, even a pillow. Tie the splint firmly in place above and below the break, but not tightly enough to cut off circulation. Use layers of cloth or newspapers to pad a hard splint.

Broken bones in the hand, arm, or shoulder should be supported by a sling after splinting. Use a triangular bandage or a substitute such as a scarf, towel, or torn width of sheet and tie the ends around the casualty's neck. Or place his forearm across his chest and pin his sleeve to his coat. In this way the lower sleeve will take the weight of the injured arm.

If you suspect a broken neck or back do not move the casualty except to remove him from further danger that may take his life. If you must remove the casualty, slide him gently onto a litter or a wide, rigid board. Then leave him alone until trained help arrives.

If a bone has punctured the skin, cover the wound with a first aid dressing or clean cloth and control bleeding by hand pressure.

IV. FOR SHOCK

TAKE THIS EMERGENCY ACTION

Shock may result from severe burns, broken bones, or other wounds, or from acute emotional disturbance. Usually the person going into shock becomes pale. His skin may be cold and moist. His pulse may be rapid. He may become wet with sweat. He may become unconscious.

Open your mouth wide and place it tightly over the casualty's nostrils shut or close the nostrils with your cheek. Or close the casualty's mouth and place your mouth over the nose. Blow into his mouth or nose. (Air may be blown through the casualty's teeth, even though they may be clenched.) The first blowing efforts should determine whether or not obstruction exists.

Remove your mouth, turn your head to the side, and listen for the return rush of air that indicates air-exchange. Repeat the blowing effort. For an adult, blow vigorously at the rate of 12 breaths per minute. For a child, take relatively shallow breaths appropriate for the child's size at the rate of about 20 per minute.

If you are not getting air-exchange, recheck the head and jaw position. If you still do not get air-exchange, quickly turn the casualty on his side and administer several sharp blows between the shoulder blades in the hope of dislodging foreign matter. Again sweep your fingers through the casualty's mouth to remove any foreign matter.

Those who do not wish to come in contact with the person may hold a cloth over the casualty's mouth or nose and breathe through it. The cloth does not greatly affect the exchange of air.

Mouth-To-Mouth Technique For Infants And Small Children

If foreign matter is visible in the mouth, wipe it out quickly with your fingers or a cloth wrapped around your fingers.

Place the child on his back and use the fingers of both hands to lift the lower jaw from beneath and behind, so that it juts out.

Place your mouth over the child's mouth and nose making a relatively leak-proof seal, and breathe into the child, using shallow puffs of air. The breathing rate should be about 20 per minute.

If you meet resistance in your blowing efforts, recheck the position of the jaw. If the air passages are still blocked, the child should be suspended momentarily by the ankles or inverted over one arm and given two or three sharp pats between the shoulder blades, in the hope of dislodging obstructing matter.

Other Manual Methods Of Artificial Respiration

Persons who cannot, or will not, use the mouth-to-mouth (mouth-to-nose) method of artificial respiration should use another manual method. The nature of the injury in any given case may prevent the use of one method, while favoring another. Other methods suggested for use by the American National Red Cross are THE CHEST PRESSURE-ARM LIFT METHOD (Silvester) and THE BACK PRESSURE-ARM LIFT METHOD (Holger-Nielsen).

When performing any method of artificial respiration, remember to time your efforts to coincide with the casualty's first attempt to breathe for himself.

Be sure that the air passages are clear of all obstructions, that the casualty is positioned in a manner that will keep the air passages clear, and that air is forced into the lungs as soon as possible.

If vomiting occurs, quickly turn the casualty on his side, wipe out his mouth, and reposition him.

When the casualty is revived, keep him as quiet as possible until he is breathing regularly. Loosen his clothing, cover him to keep him warm, and then treat for shock.

Whatever method of artificial respiration you use, it should be continued until the casualty begins to breathe for himself, or until there is no doubt that the person is dead.

VI. TO MOVE INJURED PERSONS
TAKE THIS EMERGENCY ACTION

Do NOT move an injured person except to prevent further injury or possible death. If you must move him, keep him lying down flat. Move him on a wide board, such as an ironing board or door, and tie him to it so he won't roll off.

If you have nothing to carry him on, get two other persons to help you carry. You must kneel together on the same side of the casualty and slide your hands under him gently. Then lift carefully, keeping his body level. Walk in step to prevent jarring, and carry him only far enough to remove from danger.

CURRENT CHANGES IN FIRST-AID METHODS

When an accident occurs and before medical help arrives, the victim often can be helped by someone who has knowledge of first aid. However, a person who does not know the recent developments in treatment may find that he is endangering the physical well being of the victim by using an improper method. Many of the methods once used are now obsolete. For example:

CUTS

OLD METHOD
Apply an antiseptic such as iodine, to a, cut to kill germs.

CURRENT METHOD
Wash the cut with gauze dipped in soap and water. Antiseptics can destroy living tissue around the wound and retard healing. Soap and water, however does not destroy tissue, and it provides a flushing action that washes away dirt and some bacteria.

BLEEDING FROM ARTERY

OLD METHOD
Apply a tourniquet to stop bleeding from a cut artery.

CURRENT METHOD
The best way to control any bleeding is to apply sterile compresses directly over the wound, and bandage them tightly in place. The pressure of the bandage will stem the flow of blood. Medical attention is indicated for any cut artery. The old method of using a tourniquet, say medical authorities, can be dangerous because it cuts off all circulation to the limb, which can lead to a risk of gangrene and even amputation. Also, if muscles begin to die from lack of oxygen, poisonous substances may form and get into the victim's circulation, causing "tourniquet shock."

CHOKING
CURRENT METHOD
Perform the Heimlich method by hugging the victim with his back against your body, placing your arms around his body. Make a fist with one hand, hold your fist with the other hand and place it under victim's diaphragm and forcefully push air up forcing food up windpipe and out of mouth. If necessary, make several separate forceful movements until successful.

OLD METHOD
If a person is choking, slap him on the back repeatedly in order to dislodge the obstruction.
Do nothing for a while in order to give the person's voice box (where food usually lodges) enough time to relax. At this stage the person ordinarily coughs up the object. If nothing happens and the person stops breathing, lean him forward, then slap him on the back to dislodge the obstruction. A young child may be held upside down to help dislodge any obstruction. If the obstruction can be

reached with the fingers, it should be removed. Slapping a person immediately may cause the object to be sucked, by a sudden rush of air, into his windpipe. If the object has slipped into the windpipe, a slap may make him cough, forcing the object up against the narrower opening of the vocal cords. This can cause a blockage and asphyxiation.

BURNS

OLD METHOD
When someone is burned, apply butter or other household grease to the area.

CURRENT METHOD
Never apply grease. The sterility of household greases cannot be guaranteed and therefore there is a risk of introducing infection. In serious burns, any grease or ointment must be scraped off before treatment at a hospital, and. the patient experiences more pain. If the burn is minor (one that does not require medical attention and when the skin is not broken), sterile commercial products can be used.

Another method is to submerge the burned area in cold water (under 70 degrees) and keep adding ice to maintain the temperature. Parts that cannot be submerged should be treated with a cloth dipped in cold water. Treatment should continue until the burned parts can be kept out of the cold water without recurrence of pain. However, there is still some controversy about the use of this treatment when the burn is extensive. In a serious burn, the Red Cross recommends the application of a dry sterile dressing, bandaged securely in place to protect the burn from contamination and to prevent exposure to air.

DIVING ACCIDENT

OLD METHOD
If a person diving into the water appears to have struck his head, pull him out of the water as quickly as possible.

CURRENT METHOD
Many cases of paralysis have resulted from rough handling of a person dragged out of the water. Instead, the person should be supported in the water and kept afloat until the ambulance arrives. Quite often in this type of accident, the person's neck is fractured, and moving his head roughly is likely to cause irreparable injury to the spinal cord. If, however, it is necessary to remove a person from the water, he should be placed on something rigid so that his head will be at the same level as his body.

NOSEBLEED

OLD METHOD
Use an ice pack to stop a nosebleed.

CURRENT METHOD
Tilt the person's head all the way back so that his nose becomes the highest point of his body, and pinch his nostrils. It is important to keep the head

tilted to lessen pressure. However, if the bleeding is severe, roll a piece of gauze and use it to plug his nostril, making sure that a long piece hangs out to facilitate removal. Gentle pressure can be exerted on the outside of the nostril. In severe bleeding, it is necessary to have medical attention.

POISON

OLD METHOD
Use a mixture of burned toast, tea and milk to counteract accidental swallowing of poisons.

CURRENT METHOD
Poison-control authorities say that the homemade antidote of burned toast, tea and milk is useless because the charcoal from the toast is not the kind that absorbs poisons. Call a physician immediately. Begin mouth-to-mouth resuscitation if the victim has difficulty breathing. Actually, the nature of the poison will determine the first-aid measure to use. Give water or milk. Do NOT induce vomiting if a petroleum product, such as gasoline, kerosene or turpentine has been ingested. With poisons such as an overdose of aspirin, induce vomiting by either placing a finger at the back of the victim's throat, or by giving salt water (two teaspoons to a glass) or syrup of ipecac (one ounce for adults and half an ounce for children).

ACCIDENT

OLD METHOD
Rush a person to the hospital as quickly as possible after an accident.

CURRENT METHOD
Proper carrying of an injured person is necessary in order to avoid the possibility of permanent damage. To move a person too quickly may cause spinal injury, hemorrhage or shock. Unless the person must be moved out of danger, it is BEST to apply first aid on the spot and wait until the ambulance arrives. The American Red Cross says: "The principle of first aid is to get the victim to medical attention in the best possible manner."

FIRST AID SUMMARY CHART

FOR THESE PURPOSES	USE THESE	OR THESE	SUGGESTED QUANTITY
For open wounds, scratches, and cuts. Not for burns.	1. Antiseptic Solution: Ben-zalkonium Chloride Solution, U.S. P., 1 to 1,000 parts of water.	Quaternary ammonium compounds in water. Sold under trade names as Zephiran, Phe-merol, Ceepryn, and Bactine.	3-to 6-oz . bottle.
For faintness, adult dose 1/2 teaspoon in cup of water; children 5 to 10 drops in 1/2 glass of water. As smelling salts, remove stopper, hold bottle under nose.	2. Aromatic Spirits of ammonia.		1-to 2-oz. bottle.
For shock -- dissolve 1 teaspoonful salt and 1/2 tea-spoonful baking soda in 1 quart water. Have patient drink as much as he will. Don't give to unconscious person or semiconscious person. If using substitutes dissolve six 10-gr. sodium chloride tablets and six 5-gr. sodium bicarbonate (or sodium citrate) tablets in 1 qt . water.	3. Table salt.	Sodium chloride tablets, 10 gr. , 50 tablets in bottle .	1 box.
	4. Baking soda.	Sodium bicarbonate or sodium citrate tablets, 5 gr. , 50 tablets in bottle.	8-to 10 oz. box.
For a sling; as a cover; for a dressing.	5. Triangular bandage, folded, 37 by 37 by 52 in. , with 2 safety pins.	Muslin or other strong material. Cut to exact dimensions. Fold and wrap each bandage and 2 safety pins separately in paper.	4 bandages.

FIRST AID SUMMARY CHART (Cont'd)

FOR THESE PUR-POSES	USE THESE	OR THESE	SUGGESTED QUANTITY
For open wounds or for dry dressings for burns. These are packaged sterile.	6. Two medium first aid dressings, folded, sterile with gauze enclosed cotton pads, 8 in. by 7 1/2 in. Packaged with muslin bandage and 4 safety pins.	a) Two emergency dressings 8 in. by 7 1/2 in. , in glassine bags, sterilized. One roller bandage, 2 in. by 10 yds. b) Four large sanitary napkins wrapped separately and sterilized. One roller bandage, 2 in. by 10 yards.	As indicated.
For open wounds or for dry dressings for burns. These are packaged sterile.	7. Two small first aid dressings, folded, sterile with gauze enclosed cotton pads and gauze bandage, 4 in. by 7 in.	Twelve sterile gauze pads in individual packages, 3 in. by 3 in. One roller bandage, 1 in. by 10 yards.	As indicated.
For eyes irritated by dust, smoke, or fumes. Use 2 drops in each eye. Apply cold compresses every 20 minutes if possible.	8. Eye drops.	Bland eye sold by druggists under various trade names.	1/2-to 1-oz. bottle with dropper.
For splinting broken fingers or other small bones and for stirring solutions.	9. Twelve tongue blades, wooden.	Shingles, pieces of orange crate, or other light wood cut to approximately 1 1/2 in. by 6 in.	As indicated.

FIRST AID SUMMARY CHART (Cont'd)

FOR THESE PURPOSES	USE THESE	OR THESE	SUGGESTED QUANTITY
For purifying water when it cannot be boiled. (Radioactive contamination cannot be neutralized or removed by boiling or by disinfectants.)	10.Water purification tablets Iodine (trade names-- Globa line, Burso-line, Potable Aqua) Chlorine (trade name--Halazone) .	Tincture of iodine or iodine solution (3 drops per quart of water) . Household bleach (approx . 5% available chlorine) 3 drops per quart of water.	Tablets Bottle of 50 or 100. Liquid One Small bottle.
For bandages or dressings: Old soft towels and sheets are best. Cut in sizes necessary to cover wounds . Towels are burn dressings. Place over burns and fasten with triangular bandage or strips of sheet. Towels and sheets should be laundered, ironed and packaged in heavy paper. Relaunder every 3 months.	11.Large bath towels. 12.Small bath towels. 13.Bed Sheet.		2. 2. 1.
For administering stimulants and liquids.	14.Paper drinking cups.		25 to 50.
Electric lights may go out. Wrap batteries separately in moisture-proof covering. Don't keep in flashlight.	15.Flashlight. 16.Flashlight batteries.		1. 3.
For holding bandages in place.	17.Safety pins, 1 1/2 in. lone.		12 to 15.

For cutting bandages and dressings, or for removing clothing from injured body surface.	18. Razor blades, single edge.	Sharp knife or scissors.	3.
For cleansing skin.	19. Toilet soap	Any mild soap.	1 bar.
For measuring or stirring solutions.	20. Measuring spoons.	Inexpensive plastic or metal.	1 set.
For splinting broken arms or legs.	21. Twelve splints, plastic or wooden, 1/8 to 1 1/4 in. thick, 3 1/2 in. wide by 12 to 15 in. long.	A 40-page newspaper folded to dimensions, pieces of orange crate sidings, or shingles cut to size.	As indicated.

—————